Slavery

Green Bay Center

2985 S. Ridge Rd.
Green Bay, WI 54304

[**OPPOSING
VIEWPOINTS**
DIGESTS]

Slavery

STEPHEN CURRIE

Greenhaven Press Inc., San Diego, California

Library of Congress Cataloging-in-Publication Data

Currie, Stephen, 1960–
    Slavery / Stephen Currie.
      p.   cm. — (Opposing viewpoints digests)
    Includes bibliographical references and index.
    Summary: Offers opposing viewpoints regarding the issue of slavery in the United States, discussing its historical, social, and economic aspects.
    ISBN 1-56510-880-9 (pbk. : alk. paper) — ISBN 1-56510-881-7 (lib. ed. : alk. paper)
    1. Slavery—United States—History—Juvenile literature.
2. Slavery—United States—Justification—Juvenile literature. [1. Slavery.]
I. Title. II. Series.
    E449.C975   1999
    973'.0496—dc21   98-36198
                                                         CIP
                                                          AC

Cover Photo: Library of Congress
Archive Photos: 16
Library of Congress: 21, 35, 40, 64, 85
National Archives: 39
North Wind Picture Archives: 11, 46, 69, 73, 85

©1999 by Greenhaven Press, Inc.
PO Box 289009, San Diego, CA 92198-9009

Printed in the U.S.A.

CONTENTS

FOREWORD

The only way in which a human being can make some approach to knowing the whole of a subject is by hearing what can be said about it by persons of every variety of opinion and studying all modes in which it can be looked at by every character of mind. No wise man ever acquired his wisdom in any mode but this.

—John Stuart Mill

Greenhaven Press's Opposing Viewpoints Digests in history are designed to aid in examining important historical issues in a way that develops critical thinking and evaluating skills. Each book presents thought-provoking argument and stimulating debate on a single topic. In analyzing issues through opposing views, students gain a social and historical context that cannot be discovered in textbooks. Excerpts from primary sources reveal the personal, political, and economic side of historical topics such as the American Revolution, the Great Depression, and the Bill of Rights. Students begin to understand that history is not a dry recounting of facts, but a record founded on ideas—ideas that become manifest through lively discussion and debate. Digests immerse students in contemporary discussions: Why did many colonists oppose a bill of rights? What was the original intent of the New Deal and on what grounds was it criticized? These arguments provide a foundation for students to assess today's debates on censorship, welfare, and other issues. For example, *The Great Depression: Opposing Viewpoints Digests* offers opposing arguments on controversial issues of the time as well as views and interpretations that interest modern historians. A major debate during Franklin D. Roosevelt's administration was whether the president's New Deal programs would lead to a permanent welfare state, creating a citizenry dependent on government money. *The Great Depression* covers this issue from both historical and modern perspectives, allowing students to critically evaluate arguments both in the context of their time and through the benefit of historical hindsight.

This emphasis on debate makes Digests a useful tool for writing reports, research papers, and persuasive essays. In addition to supplying students with a range of possible topics and supporting material, the Opposing Viewpoints Digests offer unique features through which young readers acquire and sharpen critical thinking and reading skills. To assure an appropriate and consistent reading level for young adults, all essays in each volume are written by a single author. Each essay heavily quotes readable primary sources that are fully cited to allow for further research and documentation. Thus, primary sources are introduced in a context to enhance comprehension.

In addition, each volume includes extensive research tools, including a section comprising excerpts from original documents pertaining to the issue under discussion. In *The Bill of Rights*, for example, readers can examine the English Magna Carta, the Virginia State Bill of Rights drawn up in 1776, and various opinions by U.S. Supreme Court justices in key civil rights cases, as well as an unabridged version of the U.S. Bill of Rights. These documents both complement the text and give students access to a wide variety of relevant sources in a single volume. Additionally, a "facts about" section allows students to peruse facts and statistics that pertain to the topic. These statistics are also fully cited, allowing students to question and analyze the credibility of the source. Two bibliographies, one for young adults and one listing the author's sources, are also included; both are annotated to guide student research. Finally, a comprehensive index allows students to scan and locate content efficiently.

Greenhaven's Opposing Viewpoints Digests, like Greenhaven's higher level and critically acclaimed Opposing Viewpoints Series, have been developed around the concept that an awareness and appreciation for the complexity of seemingly simple issues is particularly important in a democratic society. In a democracy, the common good is often, and very appropriately, decided by open debate of widely varying views. As one of democracy's greatest advocates, Thomas Jefferson, observed, "Difference of opinion leads to inquiry, and inquiry to truth." It is to this principle that Opposing Viewpoints Digests are dedicated.

The Wedge That Split the Nation

No institution in American history has been as divisive as slavery. During the first half of the nineteenth century, slavery sparked a seemingly unending number of controversies and debates—whether slavery should be permitted at all, whether the practice should be allowed in newly formed territories, whether slave revolts should be supported or suppressed, and many more. Pro- and antislavery advocates expressed positions that grew more and more extreme and increasingly ignored any middle ground. Few other issues throughout American history have so factionalized the nation geographically; few other issues have spun off into so many related debates. And, of course, no other issue in the country's existence has led to civil war.

American slavery grew up with the nation. Slavery was known in British North America since at least 1640, perhaps even earlier. By the middle of the 1600s, American ships were sailing home from Africa, carrying human cargo to be sold in the colonies. By 1670 nearly every colony permitted slavery. From its beginnings, slavery meant white masters and black slaves. Infrequent attempts to enslave Native Americans proved mainly unsuccessful, and enslaving white people was strictly forbidden. By the same token, though Native Americans and a few free blacks did own an occasional slave, the vast majority of slave owners were white.

Once established, slavery flourished. As the white population grew, so did the number of slaves. Importation of slaves from Africa continued until early in the nineteenth century, and natural increase of slaves already in America added to their numbers. By the Civil War there were perhaps 4 million slaves in the United States. They were not spread evenly across the country, however, did not perform the same sorts of tasks, and were not accorded the same treatment.

Differences Between Sections

In fact, slavery took two very divergent paths in the United States. Although every one of the original thirteen colonies permitted slavery at some point, Northern and Southern colonies developed different attitudes toward the institution. These regional differences were the foundation of many of the debates that were to come.

In most areas of the North, slavery did not prove cost-effective. The Northern economy was based on small farms and factories, and their owners found it cheaper to hire laborers to work on a day-by-day basis rather than pay for slaves' food, housing, and other needs. As a result, most Northern slaves were artisans or personal servants. Slaves were never very plentiful in the North—in 1759, for instance, only one in ten American slaves lived north of Maryland—and as time went on one Northern state after another banned slavery altogether.

In the South, however, things were different. The economy of the South depended on agriculture to a greater degree than in the North. Moreover, the climate and geography of the South made the region ideal for several crops that were difficult if not impossible to grow in the North, including rice, sugar, indigo, and, especially, cotton, crops well suited to cultivation on a large scale on big, centralized farms. This kind of production required plenty of hard labor, often year-round. Under such circumstances, slavery made sense from an economic perspective.

As a result, while Northern states were forbidding slavery, the institution was growing in the South. By the 1820s slavery

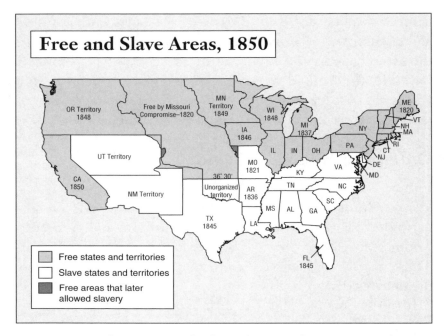

Free and Slave Areas, 1850

OR Territory
1848

Free by Missouri
Compromise–1820

MN
Territory
1849

WI
1848

ME
1820

VT

IA
1846

MI
1837

NY

NH
MA

UT Territory

IL   IN   OH   PA

RI

CT

MO
1821

VA

NJ
DE
MD

CA
1850

36° 30′

KY

NM Territory

Unorganized
territory

AR
1836

TN

NC

SC

MS   AL   GA

TX
1845

LA

FL
1845

Free states and territories

Slave states and territories

Free areas that later
allowed slavery

was more or less entrenched in the Southern states, despite the fact that most white Southerners did not themselves own slaves. Fewer than half of white adult male Southerners owned any slaves at all. Most who did owned only a few—less than ten, often less than five, and sometimes only one or two. About half the slaves lived on plantations housing twenty slaves or more, but those plantations represented only a small fraction of the slave owners of the South.

The Lives of Slaves

It is difficult to generalize about the lives of slaves. The distance between farms, the fact that so many slaves lived on fairly small plantations, and the geographical range among the slave states all led to major differences in treatment and experience. A slave on a large cotton plantation in Mississippi did not lead the same life as a slave on a small farm in Virginia. Being a house slave of a wealthy family was quite different from being a field hand whose master earned barely enough money to get by. Some slaves were comparatively well treated.

Others were the victims of horrifying abuse. Nevertheless, a few major similarities stand out.

First, all slaves, by definition, were property. They were owned. They could be sold at the whim of their master; they could be beaten for any offense at all. Legally, their children did not belong to them but to their masters. A slave could not choose his job or decide for whom she wanted to work. Slaves were given whatever food and housing their masters could afford or wanted to give them. Second, flight was a serious offense. A runaway slave often had to travel by night or hide in forests and swamps for days, even months. Slaveholders took the loss of their "property" seriously and typically went to considerable effort to recover missing slaves. "I have two of the finest dogs for catching Negroes in the Southwest," read a newspaper ad before the Civil War. "They can take the trail twelve hours after the Negro has passed, and catch him with ease."[1]

The American South was rural and depended on manual labor to harvest and plant crops. Black slaves performed almost all of this labor.

Yet in many ways the differences were more striking than the similarities. In some areas, large plantations, essentially factories for producing farm products, were the rule. Twenty, fifty, a hundred or more slaves lived together, forming what amounted to small villages. Their daily routine was rarely broken: endless marches to and from the fields, backbreaking labor all day long. On plantations with many slaves, hired overseers rather than masters tended to be in charge; likewise, rules were firm and punishment for breaking them could be severe. Owners of large plantations often gave slaves a prescribed number of strokes with a whip for various offenses. Other common punishments included imprisoning slaves in stocks or in jails, giving offenders extra work, or withholding food.

In addition to field slaves were so-called house slaves, who typically spent their time in the masters' homes on larger plantations. House slaves functioned as domestic servants, filling such jobs as coachman, seamstress, laundry worker, nursemaid, and personal servant. They spent much of their time indoors, tended to perform much less strenuous duties, and came into contact with the white people of the estate on a regular basis. These perceived advantages often led to resentment of house slaves by field slaves and a feeling of superiority among house slaves. Such disunity was good for the master; divisions among the slaves helped keep the peace on the plantation, in that the slaves would be less likely to join forces to plot against him.

In contrast, some masters owned only a handful of slaves and were more likely to work beside their slaves in the fields. On smaller farms, a slave sometimes enjoyed more opportunity to make choices, take on responsibility, or even to bend the rules. On the other hand, slaves who worked on such farms were often isolated from other blacks. Moreover, those who had a particularly vengeful master may have suffered even more than slaves on larger plantations. Many planters cultivated a good reputation in the community, and it was easier for a farmer on a small, remote plantation to abuse a slave undetected than it would have been for a more prominent landowner.

Hard, Brutal, and Short

All slaves, house or field, on large plantations or small farms, knew the feeling of not being their own masters. No matter how much responsibility they were given, no matter how well they ate, all were property in the eyes of the law. Many slaves, if not most, were sold to a new owner at some point during their lives. That sale might mean separating husbands and wives, parents and children, forever. Many were beaten for little reason, or were refused rest or treatment when seriously ill. Typically, slaves were illiterate—indeed, during much of the history of slavery it was forbidden to teach a slave how to read and write—and they were severely limited in the possessions they were allowed. Slavery was often a hard, brutal, and short life.

Slaves turned for strength to age-old comforts despite the physical and emotional pain slavery brought them. Music was one; when they could, slaves often sang in the fields as they worked. Religion was another; not all masters approved of religious services for slaves, but many Africans quickly became Christians and made that religion their own. Slaves told stories, often about weak and defenseless animals who lived by their wits and managed to defeat stronger and more powerful enemies. Slaves also became as independent as they dared by planting vegetable gardens or learning to read and write in secrecy.

Finally, slaves tested the limits of the system they lived in as much as possible. Slave owners often complained that their slaves were lazy; for the most part this was a calculated response to slavery, a subtle strike that made masters grumble but that they were powerless to stop. A few slaves arranged their own sale to other masters, or sabotaged a proposed sale by being difficult or even violent. And when blacks were given responsibility, they often used it on their own behalf. A few masters, for instance, assigned slaves to carry out whippings. "When massa was there," one man reported of the slave who had this job at a Virginia plantation, he would lay it on, because he had to. But when ol' massa wasn't, he never would beat them slaves. Would tie the slave up to one post and lash another one. Of course, the slave would scream and yell to satisfy massa, but he wasn't getting no lashing.[2]

Early Controversies

The first major controversies surrounding slavery appeared during the Revolutionary War. The colonists relied heavily on the rhetoric of "natural rights" in their war against England: They believed that people were born with inherent rights that no one was entitled to take from them. For many colonists, including some slave-owning Southerners, it was troubling to fight a war for "natural rights" and then deny those same rights to black Americans. There was enough concern about slavery among revolutionary leaders that Thomas Jefferson inserted an antislavery passage in an early draft of the Declaration of Independence, though the passage was deleted before the document was approved.

Slavery remained somewhat controversial in the new nation after American independence was achieved. The debate reflected a clear split along sectional lines: For the most part, Northerners were uncomfortable with slavery and wanted to restrict it, while Southerners preferred to let it flourish. The two sides compromised—the first of many compromises over the next seventy-five years. Under the agreement, slavery was allowed to continue, but no more Africans could be brought into the country after 1808. Runaway slaves were to be returned to their masters, even if they escaped to Northern states. Certain territories were to be closed to slavery. For purposes of representation in Congress, a slave was to be counted as three-fifths of a person.

These compromises temporarily satisfied Northerners and Southerners alike. The founders of the new government had sidestepped slavery as an obstacle to the formation of the United States. Unfortunately, however, they had failed to settle any of the fundamental questions surrounding slavery. Slavery was more a regional institution than ever, guarded zealously by the South and increasingly scorned by the North. By not deciding once and for all what to do about slavery, the nation's founders simply pushed the issue onto a new generation.

Abolitionists

By the 1830s, this generation had come of age. Led by minister Theodore Weld and journalist William Lloyd Garrison, a loud and uncompromising movement against slavery was rising in the North. Weld, Garrison, and others called themselves abolitionists because they were hoping for the abolition of slavery. They believed in immediate freedom for all slaves. Weld and Garrison did not hesitate to call slavery evil and slaveholders wicked. They brought religious and ethical arguments into play. They enraged Southerners by making speeches and distributing literature that seemed to encourage slaves to revolt. They cataloged brutalities suffered by the slaves at the hands of their masters, and they devoted their considerable energies to urging education, emancipation, and tolerance for Southern blacks.

Not all Northerners went along with the abolitionists, however. Many, perhaps most, Northerners felt that slavery was none of their business. As long as they were not confronted by it on a daily basis, it was of no concern to them what slaveholders chose to do with their property. Few white Northerners of the time believed that the black man was the equal of the white; even in the North, free blacks were discriminated against in housing and jobs, and often had fewer rights than white citizens. While few Northerners actively supported slavery, many were put off by the tone and intensity of those who worked for immediate emancipation, as well as by the comparative tolerance that many abolitionists showed toward blacks.

Yet there were a number of white Northerners who did disapprove of slavery, even if they were not entirely in the same camp as Weld and Garrison. These moderates tended to

William Lloyd Garrison was a prominent abolitionist who edited and published the antislavery journal The Liberator *from 1843 to 1865.*

adopt a more practical approach; they dismissed the notion of immediate freedom for slaves as unrealistic and worked, instead, for gradual emancipation, or freedom to be implemented slowly, over a period of years. They urged that Northern leaders work with, not against, moderate Southerners, being careful not to lose these valuable allies in a war of angry words. Concerned about the prospect of freed blacks roaming the countryside after abolition, either unable or unwilling to work for pay, many moderate abolitionists suggested that blacks ought to be returned to Africa. Though opposed to slavery, these abolitionists were scarcely friends to black Americans.

Southern Attitudes

At the same time, and partly in response, Southern attitudes toward slavery were shifting as well. While early Southerners had tended to view slavery as a necessary evil, by the 1830s Southern leaders were inclined to see it more as a positive good. The literature of the abolitionists upset many Southerners who contended that the abolitionists did not understand slavery at all; perhaps worse, they saw the abolitionists' work as an attempt to interfere in their lives. Some Southerners feared that the abolitionist movement was a sign of the Northern desire to crush the South economically and politically.

What made Southerners most uncomfortable, though, was the threat of slave revolts. Some abolitionists openly encouraged slaves to rebel against their masters. Others, many Southerners suspected, supported that goal without actually saying so. The idea of rebellion was frightening to many rural Southerners. Most large plantations had many more slaves than whites. Though a revolt involving more than a few plantations was unlikely, that was small comfort to a slaveholder who worried that his own slaves might try to kill him and his family as they slept. Southern states passed laws forbidding the distribution of antislavery pamphlets and books, which of course upset Northern abolitionists further.

Just as not all Northerners were abolitionists, not all whites in the South supported slavery. In some regions, such as the Appalachian Mountains, slavery was rare and not well liked. Nevertheless, Southern society was split far more along racial lines than along class lines. The Southern farmer who owned no slaves at all felt a much closer kinship with the wealthy planter than with the typical free black, let alone with the lowly slave. By law and custom, whites were considered to be superior to blacks—superior in intelligence, superior in winning privileges and rights, superior in social status. While many Southern whites did not benefit directly from slavery, very few were willing to condemn the system in any way.

Gradually, opposition to slavery within the South became harder to detect. In 1831 the slave Nat Turner led a rebellion in Virginia in which sixty whites were killed. In the panic that ensued among white Virginians, about two hundred blacks were killed as well. That same year the Virginia General Assembly debated the future of slavery in the state. Several lawmakers spoke in favor of gradual emancipation, with payments made to slave owners who gave up their property. The plan went nowhere. It was the last significant public discussion about the rightness and morality of slavery anywhere in the South.

Tensions Between Regions

With attitudes hardening on both sides, Northerners and Southerners increasingly clashed over slavery. One big issue was the future of slavery in the new western territories. In 1820 the two sides had negotiated a policy known as the Missouri Compromise. This deal admitted Missouri to the Union as a slave state, added the corresponding free state of Maine, and decreed that slavery would never be allowed west of Missouri and north of its southern border. The Missouri Compromise lasted, with misgivings on both sides, until 1854, when the Kansas-Nebraska Act repealed it. Instead, the new compromise held, new territories would decide for themselves, when they became states, whether to permit slavery or not. As westward-moving Southerners had chafed under the Missouri Compromise, many Northerners took a violent dislike to the provisions of the Kansas-Nebraska Act. The question of slavery in the territories had not been resolved, and with tensions escalating, it appeared increasingly unlikely that they could be peacefully resolved.

The question of fugitive slaves became another sticking point. Southerners insisted that slaves were property. Just as a

horse who wandered away from a farm still belonged to its owner, so too was a slave who escaped still the property of his master, even if the slave had run off to a state where slavery was prohibited. Northerners, however, grew less and less tolerant of this attitude. Having no stake in slavery, they tended to applaud a slave who had the gumption to run away; some Northerners even helped guide fugitives to safety.

In 1850 the fugitive slave laws were strengthened. Many Northerners, even those who did not personally oppose slavery, were upset by this turn of events, objecting to the laws as meddling in the business of the North. Some grew concerned that slaveholders were gaining too great a voice in the way the country was being run. Just as Southerners felt that Northerners were trying to tell them how to run their states, these Northerners—whatever their feelings about slavery itself—worried that slaveholders were assuming more power than they deserved. Like the issue of slavery in the territories, the issue of fugitive slaves had become a wedge dividing the nation.

As a result of these debates, the slavery question had transcended slavery. By 1860, whether they benefited from slavery or not, most Southerners were vocal in their support of the institution. Slavery had become a rallying cry, a way of banding an entire region together against the North and a way of establishing a regional identity. To support slavery meant supporting the South against the bullying and fearmongering of the North.

At the same time, the sentiment of much of the North was shifting toward abolitionism. Opposing slavery meant being against an immoral system, of course, but for Northerners it now meant much more. Being against slavery was a sign that a person was not willing to let the South dictate policy on every issue. To support abolition meant supporting the North against an increasingly paranoid group of Southerners determined to spread their way of life across the entire nation. By 1860 the debate over slavery had become a debate over a good deal more than slavery itself: It was shorthand for regional conflict and a struggle about whose image of the United States would prevail.

Conflict

The presidential election of 1860 was one of the most bitter in the nation's history. Abraham Lincoln, of the relatively new Republican Party, won despite the fact that he received virtually no votes from the South. Although he was no friend to slavery, Lincoln pledged not to interfere with slavery where it already existed. However, he did take a strong stand against the expansion of slavery into the western territories.

South Carolina officials decided not to wait to see what Lincoln would actually do once in office. A month after the election, South Carolina lawmakers voted to secede from the Union. They were followed by several other states, who promptly banded together to form the Confederate States of America. Lincoln, upon taking office, refused to recognize the secession. By early 1861, the Civil War had begun.

Abraham Lincoln was elected president in 1860. Although Lincoln was against slavery, he did not believe that blacks were equal to whites.

Despite pressure from many of his advisers, Lincoln refused at first to make slavery the central focus of the war. His prime objective, he said, was to save the Union by any means necessary. But as time went on, Lincoln changed his mind. He issued the Emancipation Proclamation, to take effect on the first day of January 1863. Officially, the proclamation freed all slaves under Confederate rule. In fact, however, the document had no immediate effect. Lincoln had no power to enforce his edict in Confederate-held areas. He had also deliberately excluded the border states, which had remained loyal to the Union despite allowing slavery, and the areas of the Confederacy that the Union had already won back.

Nevertheless, the point had been made. From then on, it was impossible to imagine both a Northern victory and the continuance of slavery. Soon after the war ended in 1865, Congress passed the Thirteenth Amendment to the Constitution, which abolished slavery everywhere in the United States. More than two hundred years after it had begun in the British colonies, slavery was at last gone forever.

1. Quoted in B.C. Hall and C.T. Wood, *The South*. New York: Touchstone, 1995, p. 115.

2. West Turner, quoted in Julius Lester, *To Be a Slave*, New York: Dial Press, 1968, p. 35.

CHAPTER 1

Is Slavery Defensible?

"The right to enjoy liberty is inalienable. Every man has a right to his own body—to the products of his own labor—to the protection of law—and to the common advantages of society."

Slavery Is Evil and Unjust

Slavery is an undemocratic practice that stands in direct opposition to the principles this country was founded upon. Holding people in bondage, moreover, violates natural and moral laws that pertain to all peoples in all times. "The right to enjoy liberty is inalienable," argue the members of the American Anti-Slavery Society. "Every man has a right to his own body—to the products of his own labor—to the protection of law—and to the common advantages of society."[1] Rights are not dependent on skin color—they are rights, pure and simple, and it is immoral to deny Africans the same rights as whites. "Our whole creed," writes abolitionist Charles Forten, "is summed up in this single position, that the slave is a man."[2]

We cannot award rights to some but not others. "All Men, as they are the Sons of Adam, are Co-Heirs," writes Massachusetts judge Samuel Sewall, "and have equal Right unto Liberty, and all other outward Comforts of Life."[3] It is true that individual people might, under certain circumstances, forfeit their right to remain free. A murderer or thief, for instance, may justly be imprisoned. However, this on no account implies that an entire race may be enslaved. Such a concept is shocking to human nature. No people of God should be sentenced to bondage in perpetuity, regardless of the color of their skin.

Ethics and the Golden Rule

The idea of natural rights is grounded firmly in both the Bible and in ethical and political thought. It is true that few biblical passages indicate disapproval of slavery. Exodus 21:16, however, states, "He that stealeth a man, and selleth him, or if he be found in his hand, he shall surely be put to death." What is slavery but the stealing and the sale of people?

More important, the New Testament instructs men and women alike to treat others as they would be treated by others. It is difficult to imagine any person freely choosing to live the life of a slave. Therefore, this message must be construed as opposing the enslavement of others. "The moral precepts of the Bible are diametrically opposed to slavery," writes Rhode Island minister Francis Wayland. "They are, Thou shalt love thy neighbor as thyself, and all things whatsoever ye would that man should do unto you, do ye even so unto them."[4] The second part of Wayland's remark is best known as the Golden Rule.

But slaveholders twist these principles to suit their own purposes. A man can scarcely love his neighbor by enslaving him. And surely no slaveholder would choose to change places with his slave, as the Golden Rule and other moral precepts demand. Indeed, the Golden Rule, strictly applied, would give the African equal right to enslave the master. Slavery is evil and unjust under any circumstances, but this hypocritical attitude of the masters makes it far worse. Midwestern minister Theodore Weld writes:

> Clank the chains in [the slaveholder's] ears and tell him they are for *him*. Give him an hour to prepare his wife and children for a life of slavery. Bid him make haste and get ready their necks for the yoke,

and their wrists for the coffle chains, then look at his pale lips and trembling knees, and you have *nature's* testimony against slavery.[5]

Slaveholders do not treat their slaves in the way they would wish to be treated themselves. Thus, the whole idea of slavery violates the laws of God and the laws of man.

Revolution, Democracy, and Liberty

The question of rights goes deeper, however. Americans can hardly justify keeping blacks in bondage, when their own ancestors fought the Revolutionary War to gain freedom from the English Crown. "We have boasted of our liberty and free spirit," writes one commentator. "God gave us liberty and we have enslaved our fellow men!"[6] Colonial slaveholders complained that the British trampled on their rights. In response, today's slaveholders trample on the rights of their slaves.

Indeed, slaveholders helped lead the fight for American independence based on the "natural law" that says men may govern themselves. Now, hypocritically, they ignore the same principle where the black race is concerned. "Must not every generous foreigner feel a secret indignation rise in his breast," writes a New Jersey abolitionist,

> when he hears the language of Americans upon any of their own rights as freemen being in the least infringed, and reflects that these very people are holding thousands and tens of thousands of their innocent fellow men in the most debasing and abject slavery, deprived of every right of freemen, except light and air?[7]

Similarly, slave owners defy the ideals of the Constitution and the Declaration of Independence. Once again, the rights that they hold dear for themselves they do not choose to extend to blacks. "God created all men equal," writes a free black abolitionist, James Forten, quoting the Declaration. "This idea embraces the Indian and the European, the Savage and the Saint, the Peruvian and the Laplander, the white Man and the African."[8]

Even a few Southerners agree that the basic political documents of the American people make it hard to justify slavery. S.D. Moore of Virginia, for instance, points out that slave owners deny their slaves rights that are not only "the common property of the human race" but more specifically among the "sound principles of our government."[9] Sadly, voices such as Moore's are seldom heard in the South. Nor does every Northerner accept the argument. Clearly, though, a nation which says it values liberty and the pursuit of happiness may not justly deny these ideas to a whole race.

1. Quoted in Louis Ruchames, *The Abolitionists: A Collection of Their Writings.* New York: G.P. Putnam's Sons, 1963, p. 80.

2. Quoted in Ruchames, *The Abolitionists*, p. 132.

3. Samuel Sewall, "The Selling of Joseph a Memorial," quoted in William Dudley, ed., *Slavery.* San Diego: Greenhaven Press, 1992, p. 26.

4. Quoted in William Sumner Jenkins, *Pro-Slavery Thought in the Old South.* Chapel Hill: University of North Carolina Press, 1935, p. 223.

5. Theodore Dwight Weld, *American Slavery as It Is,* quoted in Dudley, *Slavery*, p. 73.

6. Quoted in Jenkins, *Pro-Slavery Thought in the Old South*, p. 35.

7. David Cooper, "A Serious Address," quoted in Dudley, *Slavery*, p. 48.

8. James Forten, *Letters,* quoted in Dudley, *Slavery*, p. 50.

9. Quoted in Jenkins, *Pro-Slavery Thought in the Old South*, pp. 84–85.

"The patriarchs themselves, those chosen instruments of God, were slaveholders. . . . No human institution, in my opinion, is more manifestly consistent with the will of God than domestic slavery."

Slavery Is Moral and Just

As practiced by Southern slaveholders, slavery is well within the compass of morality. Evidence from history, natural law, science, and politics supports this view. But perhaps the most important argument for the essential rightness of slavery comes from Scriptures. The Bible, in truth, provides all the justification slavery needs.

According to the Old Testament, for example, the ancient Israelites held and sold slaves. At no point in the Bible does God condemn this activity. Indeed, in several passages, God is seen to encourage the Hebrews to enslave non-Jews. In Leviticus 25: 44-46, for instance, God goes further, ordaining slavery as a proper and just system:

> Both thy bondmen, and thy bondmaids, which thou shalt have, shall be of the heathen that are round about you; of them shall ye buy bondmen and bondmaids. Moreover, of the children of the strangers that do sojourn among you, of them shall ye buy, and of the families that are with you, which they begat in your land: and they shall be your possession. And ye shall take them as an inheritance for

your children after you, to inherit them for a possession; they shall be your bondmen for ever.

Nor does the New Testament override this view. Nowhere in
the Gospels does Jesus Christ ever condemn slavery, and the
apostle Paul frequently exhorts slaves to remain obedient to
their masters.

It is clear from these scriptural references that God
approves of slavery, at least where lesser races are concerned.
"The practice of the people of God in all ages," writes Massachusetts judge and slavery advocate John Saffin,

> both before and after the giving of the Law, and in
> the times of the Gospel, [was] that there were Bond
> men, Women and Children commonly kept by good
> and holy men, and improved in Service; and there-
> fore by the Command of God . . . and their venera-
> ble Example, we may keep Bond men, and use them
> in our Service still.[1]

If God ordains it, then slavery cannot possibly be an evil.
"Under both the Jewish and Christian dispensations of our
religion," writes George McDuffie, governor of South
Carolina,

> domestic slavery existed with the unequivocal sanc-
> tion of its prophets, its apostles, and finally its great
> Author. The patriarchs themselves, those chosen
> instruments of God, were slaveholders. . . . No
> human institution, in my opinion, is more manifest-
> ly consistent with the will of God than domestic
> slavery.[2]

As the literal word of God, the Bible cannot be considered
lightly or dismissed. The evidence from religion is all on the
side of slavery.

"Qualities That Fit Them for Slaves"

History offers further proof that slavery is a morally correct
way of life. The abolitionists contend that "natural law"

condemns slavery. But they misinterpret the concept. Natural law does not mean some vaguely defined concept of "justice" and "equality," for nature is scarcely equal and just in its distribution of resources. An examination of societies through time reveals the truth: Slavery is a natural condition, the usual way of things, and it has always been so. Slavery is scarcely limited to our own time and place. Far from it; slavery is a universal. "Every shade and variety of slavery has existed in the world,"[3] writes George Fitzhugh, a Southern lawyer and journalist. Enslaving others is, quite simply, a truth of history and a part of human nature. Thus, so-called "natural law," far from condemning slavery, justifies it.

Moreover, nature has made Africans obvious candidates for slavehood. Blacks cannot govern themselves without the steadying hand of the civilized slave owner. "[Africans] have all the qualities that fit them for slaves," writes McDuffie,

> and not one of those that would fit them for freedmen. They are utterly unqualified, not only for rational freedom but for self-government of any kind. . . . It is utterly astonishing that any enlightened American, after contemplating all the manifold forms in which even the white race of mankind is doomed to slavery and oppression, should suppose it possible to reclaim the African race from their destiny.[4]

Evidence for this comes from many sources. As far as the Bible is concerned, it is entirely possible that Africans are descended from Canaan, a grandson of Noah whose descendants were doomed to perpetual servitude. A careful study of political and social systems leads to the same conclusion: Africans are inferior. In every way, African society is far less complex and advanced than European society. Scientific evidence, such as comparisons of the slope of foreheads, suggests that Africans may not even be truly human, but rather a step between the whites and the great apes. Mentally, spiritually, or morally, the African is scarcely equal to the white.

Slavery Is a Positive Force

In fact, for the poor African, slavery is not a curse but a blessing. Indeed, enslavement ultimately benefits the slave. Bringing slaves here from Africa is perhaps the only way to introduce them to Christianity, thus saving their souls for all eternity. Moreover, bondage protects slaves from their baser desires and exposes them to the wisdom of their masters, thereby uplifting them. The African is ruled by instinct and animal desires rather than reason; the savage way he lives in Africa is evidence of that. The system of slavery, however, can improve the slave's fate. "Nothing but arbitrary power" such as a white slavemaster holds, says philosopher S.A. Cartwright, "can restrain the excesses of [the slave's] animal nature and restore reason to her throne."[5]

Antislavers argue that slaves have rights too. We reply: What rights? The slave is only a grown-up child, notes George Fitzhugh. Just as children, idiots, and madmen need guidance from those who are steadier or wiser, so too do slaves. "When it is said that slavery is inconsistent with human rights," writes Presbyterian minister James Henley Thornwell,

> we crave to understand what point in this line the slave is conceived to occupy. There are, no doubt, many rights which belong to other men which are denied him. But is he fit to possess them? Has God qualified him to meet the responsibilities which their possession necessarily implies?[6]

In fact, it would be cruel to follow the abolitionists' wishes and set the African free. Because slaves are incapable of reason, they will prove unable to provide for themselves. As Fitzhugh puts it, "They would be far outstripped or outwitted in the chase of free competition."[7] Each generation of slaves held in bondage, however, will benefit from that bondage. Little by little, African slaves under the steady guidance of their white masters will learn to reason, will grow in wisdom and understanding—and will become, perhaps, many decades down the road, full-fledged members of this society. In Africa, such changes could never come to pass. Slavery is surely a better fate for blacks than emancipation or leaving them in Africa could ever be.

1. John Saffin, *A Brief and Candid Answer to a Late Printed Sheet*, quoted in Dudley, *Slavery*, p. 35.

2. George McDuffie, speech in *American History Leaflets, Colonial and Constitutional*, quoted in Dudley, *Slavery*, p. 66.

3. George Fitzhugh, *Sociology for the South, or the Failure of Free Society*. Richmond, VA: A. Morris, 1854, p. 94.

4. Quoted in Dudley, *Slavery*, p. 67.

5. Quoted in Jenkins, *Pro-Slavery Thought in the Old South*, pp. 250–51.

6. Quoted in Jenkins, *Pro-Slavery Thought in the Old South*, p. 231.

7. Fitzhugh, *Sociology for the South*, p. 84.

"There is not upon the face of the earth any class of people, high or low, so perfectly free from care and anxiety. In the extremity of old age, instead of being driven to beggary or to seek public charity in a poorhouse, they will be comfortably accommodated and kindly treated among their relatives and associates."

Most Slaves Are Treated Humanely

Slavery is a fair and benevolent system. Abolitionists often complain that slavery is a brutal way of life that breaks the backs and spirits of the slaves. In truth, few slaves are brutalized, either physically or emotionally. Laws and customs restrain the occasional example of cruelty. And the slave life is a life of luxury compared with the lives of the free white laborers in the North and in the countries of Europe. While both work to enrich others, there is one essential difference: The black slave is assured a steady job and lifetime care. The freeman of the North has no such guarantee. As one thinker writes, "Slavery is a protection from pauperism."[1]

No thinking Southerner will deny that some masters have mistreated their slaves. Of course a few have done so. But then, there are brutal men in every society, and in every occupation. Among western farmers there are men who mistreat their horses—who beat them, starve them, and work them to death. Among captains of whaling ships there are men who brutalize and even murder their sailors. But it cannot be concluded from the actions of a few that farming and whaling should be stopped. Nor should it be concluded that slavery is inhumane because of the way a handful of rogue masters treat their charges.

In fact, the men who brutalize their slaves are so rare as to stand out. Moreover, they suffer the disgust of the entire community. At times they even run into legal troubles. Abolitionists who assail the record of the South like to present cases of shocking abuse without informing their audience of the aftermath. Lydia Maria Child is perhaps more honest than most; after detailing a particularly horrible case in Mississippi, she admits that "the master was universally blamed and shunned for the cruel deed."[2] So it is most of the time.

And Southern customs constrain the worst impulses of the master. Northerners often do not stop to see how this is done. An excellent example would be the sale of slaves. People in the North often grow angry over advertisements of slaves for sale. They have been told, and now believe, that every slave sold is necessarily separated from friends and family, never again to see mother or father, wife or husband, child or parent. Nothing could be further from the truth. While such a sale might well bring in more money to the pocket of a former owner, the custom of the South is to refuse such a sale if a slave can be made happier with a different owner. As a result, the vast majority of slaves who are sold stay within the same area or are sold along with family members. Nor do masters known to be brutal have an easy time buying new slaves; by tradition, community members band together to prevent this from happening.

Comparisons Between North and South

Abolitionists like to complain about whippings, but once again, they miss the point. Naturally a slave is sometimes unwilling to do what he must do; like a horse, he is then beaten until he does so. What can be the harm in that? That is not cruelty, merely a recognition of the African's inferiority and need to submit to a

Negroes for Sale.

A Cargo of very fine stout Men and Women, in good order and fit for immediate service, just imported from the Windward Coast of Africa, in the Ship Two Brothers.— Conditions are one half Cash or Produce, the other half payable the first of January next, giving Bond and Security if required.

The Sale to be opened at 10 o'Clock each Day, in Mr. Bourdeaux's Yard, at No. 48, on the Bay.

May 19, 1784. JOHN MITCHELL.

Thirty Seasoned Negroes

To be Sold for Credit, at Private Sale.

AMONGST which is a Carpenter, none of whom are known to be dishonest.

Also, to be sold for Cash, a regular bred young Negroe Man-Cook, born in this Country, who served several Years under an exceeding good French Cook abroad, and his Wife a middle aged Washer-Woman, (both very honest) and their two Children. Likewise. a young Man a Carpenter. For Terms apply to the Printer.

Advertisements announce a slave auction. In some auctions, slaves were placed on display in the nude and underwent degrading examinations by potential buyers.

master. Indeed, a moment's thought demonstrates that the master-slave relationship does not permit brutality. No thinking slave master would deliberately destroy his property by beating it half to death or working it too hard. In fact, quite the opposite is true. "The slaves are all well fed," George Fitzhugh writes, "well clad, have plenty of fuel, and are happy."[3]

What is more, the system of slavery produces far better results than the system of free labor used in the North or in Europe. Consider what happens to a slave who becomes disabled, or one who grows too old to work. He is not turned out into the cold, but given continued food and shelter by his master, who appreciates his loyal servant's years of good work. Consider what happens, in contrast, to a so-called free laborer of the North whose working life is over. He is at the mercy of his employer, who feels no loyalty or sense of duty toward an old or injured employee and is likely to set him adrift, leaving him to fend for himself. Who is better off?

The same argument applies to impoverishment. Even if a slave's master goes bankrupt, the slave will not suffer unduly. Instead of starving, he will be sold to a master who can care for him adequately. If an entire region suffers from economic distress, slaves will be sold to a wealthier region. What of the Northern wage slave? The mill owners routinely close factories and fire workers on the slimmest of pretexts. In the South, the master's first thought is of his slaves and how to protect them. Not so in the North.

The difference in living conditions between Southern slaves and laborers in "civilized" parts of Europe also argues for the gentleness of slavery. "I have traveled through most parts of Scotland and Ireland," writes a Virginia planter,

> and I can safely assert, that the habitations of the negroes are palaces and their living luxurious, when compared with those of the peasants in either of those countries. . . . The condition of the slaves is far happier than that of the Scotch or Irish vulgar.[4]

It is perhaps no surprise that life in the South is superior in so many ways to life elsewhere. The crime rate is lower, the level of social distress lower as well. We Southerners call our slaves slaves, and they benefit from knowing their place. In the North and in Europe, however, they call their wage slaves "free," at great cost to the social fabric of the land and to the workers themselves.

For the poor, slavery is the best of all possible worlds. "There is not upon the face of the earth any class of people, high or low, so perfectly free from care and anxiety," writes South Carolina's McDuffie. "In the extremity of old age, instead of being driven to beggary or to seek public charity in a poorhouse, they will be comfortably accommodated and kindly treated among their relatives and associates."[5] It is in the economic interest of the slave master to treat the slave well, while it is not in the economic interest of the employer of free men. Slavery is not only kind and benevolent, but a conscientious and humane way of providing for the poor.

1. Quoted in Jenkins, *Pro-Slavery Thought in the Old South*, p. 298.

2. Lydia Maria Child, *An Appeal in Favor of That Class of Americans Called Africans.* 1836. Reprinted New York: Arno Press, 1968, p. 29.

3. Fitzhugh, *Sociology for the South*, p. 246.

4. Quoted in Jenkins, *Pro-Slavery Thought in the Old South*, p. 40.

5. Quoted in Dudley, *Slavery*, p. 68.

"A man does not whip his horse to death if it balks or otherwise displeases him, yet too often a slave is beaten, even to death, for some equally small infraction. Slavery reduces slaves to a status below that of animals."

Most Slaves Are Treated Brutally

Slavery is a brutal system that only dehumanizes the slave. Abolitionists have compiled long lists of horrors suffered by slaves at the hands of their masters. Reports of these atrocities are not hard to find. They appear daily in the columns of almost any Southern newspaper. While a few owners do treat their slaves with gentleness and care, these few are the exception. In any case, the black man cannot choose a benevolent owner. "The negro's fate," observes activist Lydia Maria Child, "depends entirely on the character of his master."[1]

Most slave owners treat their slaves with cruelty and malice. The physical damage is most obvious. There are dozens upon dozens of cases of slaves who have been beaten, tortured, raped, and even killed—far too many for slavery supporters to dismiss as unusual. Of course, slaveholders argue that all punishments are for "just cause." Just cause, indeed: as one slave put it, "They whipped my father, because he looked at a slave they killed and cried."[2]

Slave masters use terror and the threat of terror to control their charges. Nearly every plantation has at least one slave, often more, whose back is crisscrossed with scars from repeated whippings, who was branded or whose front teeth were knocked out so that he could be easily found again if he were to run away, whose bones have been broken by masters and overseers as a penalty for some real or imaginary transgression. One traveler witnessed the flogging of a young slave woman who had been caught hiding in the bushes, perhaps to avoid work. The woman received thirty or forty blows with the whip. When the traveler questioned the severity of the punishment, the overseer replied, "If I hadn't punished her so

A young slave's back bears the scars of his master's whip. Slaves were whipped and beaten for misbehavior.

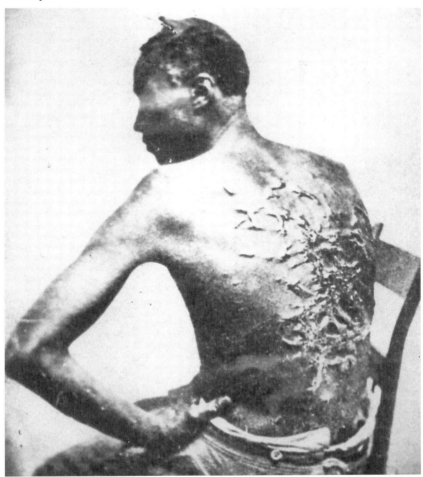

hard she would have done the same thing again to-morrow, and half the people on the plantation would have followed her example." [3] This attitude is standard throughout the South, and serves only to brutalize the slave.

Other Kinds of Brutality

But physical punishment is not the only sign of cruelty. What of children who are sold away from their parents, never to see them again? This, too, happens regularly in slave states. No law prevents it. Let the master need more money, or let another owner make a good enough offer for one member of a family, and a sale is made. A slave tells of a woman who had several children, each one sold away in turn before it reached the age of two. The woman poisoned her last baby to make sure such a fate did not befall it as well. "She got up and give it something out of a bottle," the narrator reports, "and pretty soon it was dead." [4] A system that can drive a mother to kill her own child—out of love, not out of malice—is barbarous indeed.

Other slaves may not be punished directly, but are nevertheless soon dead of overwork and inattention to medical needs.

As a black woman is auctioned off, she is forced to go with her new master and be forever separated from her son. Slave owners did not believe that blacks had the same sentiments toward their children that whites had.

No one should have to work as a slave is made to work. As former slave Solomon Northup describes life in the cotton fields,

> An hour before daylight the horn is blown. Then the slaves arise, prepare their breakfast, fill a gourd with water, in another [gourd] deposit their dinner of cold bacon and corn cake, and hurry to the field. . . . Then the fears and labors of another day begin and until its close there is no such thing as rest. . . . With the exception of ten or fifteen minutes, which is given them at noon to swallow their allowance of cold bacon, they are not permitted to be a moment idle until it is too dark to see, and when the moon is full, they oftentimes labor till the middle of the night.[5]

Once again, this sort of treatment is perfectly legal. Nor does any respectable Southerner look down on masters who require this work of their slaves. And yet slaveholders say that slavery is a kind and benevolent system!

Laws and Legal Standing

Indeed, there is little chance of redress if a master is less than kind. Admittedly, some laws are designed to prevent some of the worst kinds of brutality. But in fact these laws are often silenced by the slaveholder courts. It is exceedingly rare for a white man to be brought to trial, let alone convicted, for a crime against a slave. And it is odd that these laws are needed, if slaveholders treat their slaves as well as we are told they do. As Lydia Child points out, "If negroes have never been scalded, burned, mutilated, &c., why are such crimes forbidden by an express law?"[6]

The brutalization of slaves is such that animals in the South are often better treated than slaves. Worse still, the laws allow this disparity. "Does a man take the calf from the cow and sell it to the butcher?" asks Daniel A. Payne, a black educator and minister. "Slavery tears the child from the arms of the reluctant mother, and barters it to the slave trader."[7] A man does not whip his horse to death if it balks or otherwise displeases him, yet too often a slave is beaten, even to death, for some equally small infraction. Slavery reduces slaves to a status below that of animals. It converts a person into an object with no legal standing at all.

The fact of no legal standing is critical. If a Northern wage earner is beaten by his employer, he can take his employer to court. But if a Southern slave is mistreated, he has no recourse. He is nothing but property. Even a slave who appears well treated is still only a slave, subject to punishment at the whim of his master. Slaveholders point to these apparently happy men and women as if they were typical of the race. In fact, the truth is much sadder. Not only are they far from typical, but their condition points up the awful truth of slavery: The system allows the master to treat his servants without regard to their well-being. The kindest master can turn suddenly and thrash his slaves for no reason—and escape punishment or censure. "Despots always insist that they are merciful,"[8] Theodore Weld writes in response to those who claim that most Southern masters are kind; holding total power over another human being may, in fact, be the surest way of turning a man into a despot.

The slave system itself is wrong. It allows and even encourages brutality among slave owners. It permits masters to think of their charges as less than human. Even if all Southern masters were kind and generous to their slaves, slavery would still be an evil, for the slave-master relationship is brutal in and of itself. Not until laws are changed and slaves are freed can this terrible wrong be righted.

1. Child, *An Appeal in Favor of That Class of Americans Called Africans*, p. 29.

2. Roberta Manson, quoted in Lester, *To Be a Slave*, p. 33.

3. Quoted in Michael Mullin, ed., *American Negro Slavery: A Documentary History*. New York: Harper and Row, 1976, p. 186.

4. Lou Smith, quoted in Lester, *To Be a Slave*, p. 40.

5. Solomon Northup, *Twelve Years a Slave*. Buffalo: Miller, Orton, and Mulligan, 1854, pp. 167, 170.

6. Child, *An Appeal in Favor of That Class of Americans Called Africans*, p. 74.

7. Daniel A. Payne, speech, *Lutheran Herald and Journal*, quoted in Dudley, *Slavery*, p. 79.

8. Quoted in Dudley, *Slavery*, p. 74.

CHAPTER 2

Slavery and Abolition

"I utterly reject, as delusive and dangerous in the extreme, every plea which justifies a procrastinated and an indefinite emancipation, or which concedes to a slave owner the right to hold his slaves as property *for any limited period."*

Abolition Should Be Immediate

Slavery is a great evil and a moral wrong; all abolitionists agree on that. How then shall it be stopped? Some argue for a gradual approach, but they are misguided. The only just and effective method is to emancipate *all* American slaves at the same time—and as soon as possible. Any other approach would simply delay the end of slavery, at best, and lead to confusion, revolution, and bloodshed, at worst.

The evidence for this is clear. First, immediate abolition of slavery is a moral imperative. Since slavery is wrong, then any delay in ending it is also wrong. Slavery consigns Africans to lives of degradation, to cruelty, to ignorance, and poverty. No thinking, feeling person can accept a continuation of this. There is no excuse for waiting. To abolish slavery over time is to accept the worst excesses of slavery for now and for the foreseeable future.

It is well to remember that slaves are stolen people, kidnapped from Africa and held in bondage ever since without right or justification. One does not cure an evil by allowing the evil to continue, even if only at reduced levels. No, one must attack an evil head on, with the intention of defeating,

Africans march to market to be sold as slaves. Some African tribes benefited from slavery by kidnapping members of other tribes and selling them to white slavers.

not accommodating, it. "I utterly reject, as delusive and dangerous in the extreme," writes abolitionist William Lloyd Garrison, "every plea which justifies a procrastinated and an indefinite emancipation, or which concedes to a slave owner the right to hold his slaves as *property* for any limited period."[1] Such a plea represents a surrender of the worst kind.

Indeed, the gradual approach has not worked in the South. George Washington and Thomas Jefferson, along with most of the founding fathers, believed that slavery would eventually wither and die of unprofitability. They were wrong. They did not anticipate the degree to which slavery would insinuate itself into Southern society. Today, virtually no one dares to raise a voice against it anywhere in the region. True, gradual emancipation was successful in the North, but the North never had the numbers of blacks nor the labor-intensive agricultural economy of the South. "We are told that the Southerners will of themselves do away with slavery," writes Lydia Maria Child. "But it is an obvious fact that all their measures have tended to perpetuate the system."[2] The supporters of gradualism play into the hands of the slaveholders, who do not wish to do away with slavery.

Averting Violence

Immediate emancipation has been accomplished elsewhere, with no alarming effects. On the Caribbean island of Santo Domingo, all slaves were freed at once and suddenly, during a civil war. The process did not lead to disaster; far from it. Blacks remained on plantations, working hard for their former masters or for themselves, and were peaceful. The only problems came later, when there was an attempt made to reenslave those newly free. A similar course of events occurred in the South American nation of Colombia. On Antigua and Bermuda in the Caribbean Sea, on the other hand, the transition to freedom was abrupt and did not involve war. There, too, the transition went smoothly. "Not the least difficulty or disorder occurred," reads Garrison's account of one such transition. "Servants found masters, masters hired servants—all gained homes, and at night scarcely an idler was to be seen."[3] Those who argue that immediate abolition must lead to violence are quite wrong.

In fact, immediate emancipation is the best way of reducing the threat of violence from slaves. Give slaves their freedom, and they will no longer be resentful of white Southerners, resentful perhaps to the point of revolt or murder. Many Southerners walk nervously around their own properties, fearful of what angry and desperate slaves may do. "Why does the white mother quake at the rustling of a leaf?" asks abolitionist Elizur Wright:

> Why, but that she is conscious that there are those around her, who have been deeply enough provoked to imbrue [soak] their hands in her blood, and in that of the tender infant of her breast? . . . Well enough she knows, that were *she* subjected to the same degradation to which she subjects others, vengeance would fire her heart, and seek the first occasion to do its fellest [cruelest] deed.[4]

Immediate emancipation would eliminate the danger at once. The relationship between slaves and masters would change to a relationship between employer and employee. The slaves would no longer rankle at being owned, at being unable to make choices of their own. They would no longer feel the need to rampage, destroy, and even kill.

Freedom, too, will bring out the best in slaves—to the benefit not only of the slaves themselves, but also their masters. Slaves will work harder if paid. They will labor more thoroughly and more carefully if they know they will be rewarded for good work, not merely punished for bad. The end of slavery, if it occurred tomorrow, would not result in large bands of wild Africans wandering the South, looting and pillaging at will. Rather, it would simply change the morality of the relationship between slave and master, safeguarding the rights of both. Most former slaves would no doubt continue to work for their former masters, but in a connection to which few could object.

What Abolition Does *Not* Mean

Although immediate abolition would enable former slaves to keep old jobs or find new ones, it does not mean that the blacks would vote, or otherwise become equal with whites—at least, not at first. It is unreasonable to expect a people kept ignorant by law for many decades to move seamlessly into white society. Mere freedom is not enough. Hand in hand with emancipation, the slaveholder must "at once begin to make amends for the past," writes Amos A. Phelps,

> by entering heartily on the work of qualifying [the slaves] for, and elevating them to all the privileges and blessings of freedom and religion;—thus doing what he can to emancipate them from their ignorance, degradation, &c.—in other words, from the *consequences* of slavery, as well as from the thing itself.[5]

Immediate emancipation, coupled with efforts such as these, will prove to be the slave owner's best insurance against revolution and violence.

A more gradual emancipation process will inevitably bog down in petty disagreements and details. Who shall decide which slaves will be freed first? Who shall decide how many shall be freed each year? Shall it be accomplished by freeing every slave in certain states first, and if so, which ones? Shall all masters part immediately with a certain percentage or fixed number of their slaves? Given the differing situations and interests of Southerners, it is difficult to imagine that these questions can be settled to everyone's satisfaction. More likely, some will cry foul, and no plan will ever be agreed upon.

It is equally easy to imagine a gradual process sabotaged by slave owners. If they are permitted to choose the slaves who will be freed first, they are apt to choose the least useful on their plantations: the old, the sick, the violent, and the weak. These men and women will be unable to find work for pay. They will become wards of the state, drifting from town to town; they will be crowded into restricted regions and will be kept away from their families and friends, under suspicion of corrupting them. Then there will be violence and bloodshed, and the laws will clamp down once again, souring our few Southern sympathizers on abolition and delaying freedom even more for the remaining slaves.

Immediate emancipation is the only moral and just way to end slavery. Compromise is impossible. That which is evil is evil. Only through swift and decisive action can the evil of slavery be destroyed.

1. William Lloyd Garrison, "Thoughts on African Colonization," quoted in Dudley, *Slavery*, p. 174.

2. Child, *An Appeal in Favor of That Class of Americans Called Africans*, p. 211.

3. Quoted in Dudley, *Slavery*, p. 180.

4. Elizur Wright, *The Sin of Slavery and Its Remedy*, quoted in John L. Thomas, *Slavery Attacked: The Abolitionist Crusade*. Englewood Cliffs, NJ: Prentice-Hall, 1965, pp. 12–13.

5. Amos A. Phelps, *Lectures on Slavery and Its Remedy*, quoted in Dudley, *Slavery*, p. 179.

*"Our own security, nay, our very existence, might be
endangered by the hasty adoption of any measure for the
immediate relief of the whole of this unhappy race."*

Abolition Should Be Gradual

It would be wonderful if immediate emancipation had a
chance of succeeding. Every abolitionist worth the name
would rejoice at the sight of hundreds of thousands of slaves
becoming free men and women, paid hired hands, and either
entering into contracts with their former masters or returning
to Africa. But for many reasons immediate freedom is an
unrealistic and impractical hope. Thus, it is our duty to support the next best measure—gradual emancipation.

Perhaps the most important argument for gradualism lies in
the South itself and its white inhabitants. It is the South that
would bear the burden of abolition, the South that has, over
the years, developed an economic system based on slavery, the
South that now has several million uneducated black slaves.
Any plan for emancipation must therefore take into account
the views of the white Southerner. It is simply not reasonable
to expect the South to instantly change its views on slavery
and its whole way of life. Its people must have time—time to
adjust their way of thinking to a slaveless society, time to make
other arrangements for housing, paying, and hiring their
workers. These changes cannot occur all at once, no matter
how much we may wish them to.

Worse, the mind of the South is strongly against immediate emancipation. Southern voices for abolition are nearly all voices for a slow process in which Southerners themselves take the lead. The reality is that the South is fond of its slave system, immoral though it may be. Southerners do not take kindly to Northerners telling them what to do and how to do it, any more than we Northerners would relish having Southerners tell us how they would like us to run Illinois or New Hampshire. Southerners fear that abolition will mean hordes of angry black men and women storming their towns and laying waste to their countrysides. Southerners are alarmed by the prospect of emancipation bringing about economic ruin.

All these concerns can be countered, but only by listening to Southern fears and worries. Southerners know slavery inside and out, and they know what plantation owners will and will not accept. Writes reformer Frances Wright:

> Any plan of emancipation, to be effectual, must consult at once the pecuniary interests and prevailing opinions of the southern planters, and bend itself to the existing laws of the southern states.[1]

Northerners may shout all they like about immediate emancipation, but that idea will never succeed until Southerners themselves see the necessity for it, which will likely not occur until the groundwork has been carefully laid.

Secession and War

The immediatists do not listen to Southern concerns. At times, more radical abolitionists seem to be trying to drive the South from the Union. Their message is an angry one, full of what one man has called "language of reproach and vituperation," which can never "win men over to the love and belief of the truth."[2] Men such as Henry David Thoreau, who oppose every attempt to work with the slave states on their own terms, seem more interested in keeping themselves "pure" than in solving the slavery problem; they would prefer that the nation separate rather than last one day longer with slavery.

Indeed, the most likely outcome of repeated calls for imme-diate abolition is secession, as Southerners realize that Northern abolitionists are not interested in working with them to solve the slavery problem. Secession, however, will leave abolitionists with no authority to do anything whatever about slavery. And secession could even lead to war if the North decides to fight to save the Union. If Southerners hear only a steady stream of insulting language, then bloodshed may result. In contrast, a message of gradual abolition, with a plan that takes into account Southern fears and deals with them respectfully, will find a willing audience in the South, avoiding war and ultimately freeing all the slaves. There is no purpose in attempting more than we can effect.

Gradualism can work. Gradual abolition can and will bring about change. It already has, in the North and in many other places where slavery was once allowed and exists no longer. In most Northern states, laws freed all African children born after a certain date, or set a certain age by which all slaves could expect to earn their freedom. Within a generation or so after the American Revolution, slavery was no more, in Connecticut, in Pennsylvania, in New Hampshire. Similar methods have rid other nations of slavery as well.

Emancipation Strategies

The same strategies can reduce slavery in the South. Several Southerners have proposed plans which are designed to do just this, within the context of the South's own particular experience. A Virginian named St. George Tucker, for instance, has suggested a system that gives slaveholders and slaves many years to adjust to all the necessary changes. "Let every female born after the adoption of the plan be free," he writes, "and transmit freedom to all her descendants, both male and female."[3] Within two generations, nearly all slaves would be free. Would it take time? Yes, of course. Could the plan be successful? Again, yes. Tucker, a Southerner, knows what his people will and will not accept, and he has invented a plan that will allay their fears.

Other plans could work as well. Another Southerner, Hinton Helper, has recommended that slavery ought not be formally abolished at all. Rather, in Helper's system the possession of slaves would be severely taxed, and the proceeds from the taxes would go directly to the blacks themselves to help them in their new life of freedom. This plan makes it in the owners' interest to eliminate slavery as quickly as possible, without demanding an instant change. The initial taxes would begin fairly low but rise quickly. "If slavery is not totally abolished" within ten years, Helper writes, "the annual tax ought to be increased from forty to one hundred dollars."[4] If Helper's plan as it stands is not acceptable to the South, then by all means vary it: Make the taxes lower, their rise less sharp, but do not ignore the Southerners' point of view.

Education, Danger, and Change

Gradual emancipation works well for other reasons. As many Southerners have pointed out, the critical flaw of immediate emancipation is the notion that freed blacks will be able to take their place in society. Nothing could be further from the truth. Uneducated as they are, the slaves will need instruction before they can be freed. It is not right, as Ralph Gurley puts it, "that men should possess that freedom, for which they are entirely unprepared, and which can only prove injurious to themselves and others."[5]

This education ought to come first. It is unfair to masters and slaves to expect instant abolition to work without it. Nor is it realistic. Even if Southerners were well disposed to the idea of emancipation, they would surely be justified in refusing to consider the prospect of mobs of immoral, ignorant, and idle blacks despoiling their plantations. "Our own security," writes Tucker, "nay, our very existence, might be endangered by the hasty adoption of any measure for the immediate relief of the whole of this unhappy race."[6]

Another question is that of compensation for the slaves. Can the government pay compensation for all slaves at once? Of course not. But it is not lawful, and may not be moral, to deprive Southerners of their property rights without fair payment. The economics of the South would make releasing slaves all at once an undue burden on owners. It is only reasonable to allow masters a chance to plan. Better to give the South time to prepare for the end of slavery; better to allow the South to determine the course of abolition. Any other approach is doomed to failure, secession, or war.

1. Frances Wright, *A Plan for the Gradual Abolition of Slavery in the United States,* quoted in Dudley, *Slavery,* p. 170.

2. Quoted in P.J. Staudenraus, *The African Colonization Movement 1816–1865.* New York: Columbia University Press, 1961, p. 203.

3. St. George Tucker, *A Dissertation on Slavery,* quoted in Dudley, *Slavery,* p. 169.

4. Hinton Helper, *The Impending Crisis,* quoted in Thomas, *Slavery Attacked,* p. 161.

5. Quoted in Staudenraus, *The African Colonization Movement,* p. 203.

6. Quoted in Dudley, *Slavery,* p. 167.

"[Colonization] has taught us how we may be relieved of the curse of slavery in a manner cheap, certain, and advantageous to both the parties."

Deporting Slaves to Africa Will Help End Slavery

Perhaps the greatest obstacle to the abolition of slavery is the question of what will become of the former slaves. Serious discussions of abolition often sidestep this problem, yet without considering it abolition is a forlorn hope at best. The primary issue is this: Emancipation, whether immediate or gradual, will result in the overrunning of the South by millions of freed blacks, nearly all without education, without marketable skills, and without any real sense of how to keep themselves alive. At the present time there are 4 million black slaves in the South, 4 million black men and women who, with emancipation, will be given equal rights and privileges with whites.

This is an intolerable situation for the white majority. Most white Southerners believe that slaves are lazy and selfish. South Carolina governor George McDuffie speaks of their "intellectual inferiority" and "natural improvidence [lack of foresight]."[1] Southern blacks who are already freed are among the poorest and most miserable people anywhere in the world. They are far from ready for equality with whites. Moreover, emancipation could present a danger to whites. Blacks too often have a tendency toward savagery and violence, and they may well be vengeful toward their former masters, especially as they prove incapable of earning a living. Under these circumstances, no sensible Southerner could be expected to approve of emancipation.

Fortunately, however, there is a solution. If all slaves, once freed, were to be immediately transported back to Africa, the major objection to abolition would be instantly removed. Assure Southerners, slaveholders and nonslaveholders alike, that blacks will not remain in America but return to their homeland, and the abolition movement can count on the support of many Southern whites. These plans, often called colonization efforts because the newly freed slaves will establish new colonies of English speakers in Africa, have already been implemented on a small scale, mainly with freed blacks; it will only take an extra push for the plan to be applied to one group of slaves, and ultimately to all slaves.

Nonslaveholding Southerners

It is well to remember that not all Southerners have a direct stake in slavery. The majority of white Southern farmers own no slaves at all, and when tradesmen and merchants are considered as well, it is quite clear that well over half of all Southerners derive no benefit from slaveholding whatsoever.

These men and women know better than anyone else how the institution of slaveholding drags the entire South down. They see firsthand how it enriches the few at the expense of the many, how it breaks the spirit of the blacks for the benefit of the masters. They see how the moral pressure of Europe and the North puts the South always on the defensive. They see how slavery and reliance on slave labor has depressed the Southern economy and prevented it from taking advantage of manufacturing opportunities, keeping it a backward region economically as well as socially. Yet, for the most part, even nonslaveholders continue to support the institution.

Why? Not out of any great love for it; simply because they see clearly how abolition will affect them. While they will not lose any slaves themselves, a general emancipation would force whites and blacks together into an equality that is untenable to most whites. Even nonslaveholders disapprove of their sons and daughters mixing with the sons and daughters of former slaves. Maryland senator Robert Goodloe Harper's characterization of blacks is commonly felt throughout the South:

> Be their industry ever so great, and their conduct ever so correct, whatever property they may acquire, or whatever respect we may feel for their characters, we never could consent . . . to see the two races placed on a footing of perfect equality with each other.[2]

Colonization

But remove the possibility of mixing by removing the freed slaves, and many Southerners, especially those without slaves themselves, will find their way clear to supporting abolition. The prospect of colonization schemes already intrigues many Southerners. As Robert Breckinridge, a Kentucky minister, phrases it: "[Colonization] has taught us how we may be relieved of the curse of slavery in a manner cheap, certain, and advantageous to both the parties."[3] Even some slaveholders agree. "Many persons," writes Harper of Southern slaveholders,

> who are now restrained from manumitting [freeing] their slaves by the conviction that they would generally become a nuisance when manumitted in [this] country, would gladly give them freedom, if they were to be sent to a place where they might enjoy it usefully to themselves and to society.[4]

And indeed colonization is both cheap and certain. As Harper indicates, many slaveholders would enlist in such a scheme simply to be rid of their slaves once and for all. Some would not even ask compensation for loss of their property. "There are a number of slaveholders," says a slave owning gentleman from Virginia, "who would voluntarily surrender their slaves, if the State would provide the means of colonizing them elsewhere."[5] Others, he adds, would gladly sell their slaves to the government for export at half their value. Collections have already been undertaken in many large cities, each bringing in hundreds or even thousands of dollars to help return the African to his home.

A total of perhaps $1.5 million a year over the next fifty years would be needed to remove all blacks from American soil. The federal government can fund this easily. In fact, the cost would not even be that great, for the gains to American society would be far greater: greater productivity; less time lost to lazy, injured, and idle slaves; a healthier moral and economic climate. Just as ships brought the black men and women to this continent, so too can ships remove them.

Benefits to Slaves

Deporting slaves to Africa would be beneficial to slaves as well. Blacks were never meant for America. Their natural home is Africa. At best, slaves who are freed and remain in America will be second-class citizens, unwanted and unappreciated. They will be doomed to wander from town to town, living a rude and corrupt existence—free in name, but in reality enslaved to the forces of prejudice and racial differences.

But sail the freedmen and women back to their native shores and they can at last be happy. They will be far from the hostility of whites. They can set up their own society, bringing American civilizing influences to the jungles where their own people live. In his ancestral homeland, free from prejudice, the black man will once again be his own master. Blacks recognize their stake in colonization. "Freedom will result injuriously," writes a group of forty free blacks in Washington, "unless there shall be opened to colored people a region, to which they may immigrate."[6]

Colonization of slaves is practical. It has many advantages for the slave and for our society as a whole. But its greatest virtue is that it provides a way to make abolition conceivable, even desirable, to Southerners.

1. Quoted in Dudley, *Slavery*, p. 66.

2. Quoted in Dudley, *Slavery*, p. 182.

3. Quoted in Staudenraus, *The African Colonization Movement*, p. 144.

4. Quoted in Dudley, *Slavery*, p. 189.

5. Thomas R. Dew, "Review of the Debate in the Virginia Legislature," quoted in Eric McKitrick, ed., *Slavery Defended: The Views of the Old South.* Englewood Cliffs, NJ: Prentice-Hall, 1963, p. 25.

6. Petition to Congress, April 1862, quoted in Ira Berlin et al., *Free at Last.* New York: New Press, 1992, p. 39.

"Even if every slave and every slaveholder wished it, removing all slaves to Africa would be an impossible task, prohibitive in its expense and overly complex in its design."

Deporting Slaves to Africa Will Not Help End Slavery

Slavery will not and cannot be ended by deportation for one very simple reason: Colonization is completely impractical. Even if every slave and every slaveholder wished it, removing all slaves to Africa would be an impossible task, prohibitive in its expense and overly complex in its design. And since neither every slave nor every slaveholder desires colonization, the task is made that much more difficult. Idealists may talk all they like about colonization, but the fact is that if slavery is to be ended, it will not be through deportation.

Supporters of colonization say the process could easily be done, and for little expense. They are wrong. They like to point to the success of the colonization societies that have already transported some free blacks back to Africa. But consider the facts. In the fifteen years leading up to 1836, American colonization societies transported fewer than three thousand freed blacks, and virtually no slaves, to new lives in Africa. Shipping even this number is already a strain on the resources of the societies. Simply to keep up with the natural increase in the numbers of slaves, colonizers would have to begin shipping over seventy thousand slaves a year.

Costs

The expenses of such an undertaking are staggering. The ships alone would be costly, especially once supplies, salaries of crews, and the like are factored in. Slaves will need to reach the ships from points far from the ocean, and this trip, too, must be paid for. Money would be needed as well to set up the colonies in Africa. No government, no private enterprise, has the resources (or the desire) to spend the thousands of dollars such a venture would surely take. At best, some slaves would be sent, and then the money would be gone, and several years would pass before more deportations could take place. In that time, the slave population would grow again, owing to natural increase, and the effort to end slavery no further along than when it began.

The costs described above do not even take into account money needed to compensate slave owners for their property. It may be true that some slaveholders would indeed release their slaves for nothing, if only someone would take them far away, but that seems an uncommon prospect. Perhaps a few wealthy gentleman planters in Virginia and South Carolina can release their slaves for no compensation and never feel the loss. For most small farmers, however, the slave represents a major investment. Just as a Northern farmer would not agree to give his horse or plow away and get nothing in return, so too will the bulk of Southerners refuse to give up their slaves unless handsomely compensated.

Moreover, the economic system of the South relies upon slavery. Without slaves, the whole system could come crashing down. Though the owners cry that slaves are lazy, that slaves are more trouble than they are worth, planters have no one else to work all day picking cotton in the hot sun. Even a proslavery thinker such as political economist Thomas Dew admits as much. "Let any farmer in Lower Virginia ask himself how many [slaves] he can spare from his plantation," he writes, "and he will be surprised to see how few can be dispensed with."[1] The owners of the South are shrewd businessmen. They will demand payment for their property and will refuse to relinquish their slaves until paid, and paid well, for otherwise they will face economic ruin. Dew estimates the value of all Southern slaves to be at least $400 million.

Practicalities and Moralities

Suppose, however, that sufficient funds could be raised—money for ships and for compensation, and for all the other items that deportation would require. Would that guarantee the end of slavery? Of course not; there are still too many practical issues to consider. There is no possibility that all slaves could be deported in the same month or even year. Imagine the burden on coastal towns as thousands upon thousands of freed blacks crowd into them with but one hope: a berth on a ship to Africa. If there were ever a recipe for violence in the South, this is it.

But if slavery would not end all at once, then how would colonization proceed? Farm by farm, county by county, or state by state? Would each plantation lose a certain percentage of slaves each year? Each system has its drawbacks. The utmost care would have to be taken to deport family groups together; otherwise, we would be as bad as the slaveholders are now in their willingness to separate husbands, wives, and children for their own ends.

Other problems arise. No one knows if Southern plantations can attract white workers to take the place of slaves. No one knows if whites could handle the conditions. If they cannot—and Southerners typically assert that they cannot—then a black market in slaves would soon develop. The price of the remaining slaves would go up, owners would be extremely reluctant to give up their servants for any reason, the South would again resist attempts at abolition, and colonization will have come to nothing.

What Slaves and Masters Really Think

Deportation would be one matter if slaves and slaveholders were truly united in support of the plan. If this were so, then colonization would be at least conceivable. Slaveholders would put pressure on one another to rid themselves of their slaves, whether compensation were available or not, and slaves would go willingly to the ships for a return to Africa. But this is not the case. Many slaveholders, perhaps most, oppose—often bitterly—the idea that slavery is wrong. To some, slavery is a positive force, an institution they respect and require. "Domestic slavery," writes George McDuffie, "is the cornerstone of our republican edifice [structure]."[2] "I hold [slavery] to be a good, as it has thus far proved itself to be,"[3] agrees South Carolina senator John Calhoun. It is not reasonable to expect men and women with such strong beliefs to fall into line with the colonization movement. Slavery is too precious to them.

A similar argument applies to the blacks themselves. Although they were brought here against their will, slaves and freed blacks are Americans now. "Africa is no more their native country than England is ours," writes Lydia Maria Child. "Nay, it is less so, because there is no community of language or habits."[4] Indeed, most free blacks do not wish for deportation. A group of black freedmen protests colonization schemes as follows:

> Whereas our ancestors (not of choice) were the first successful cultivators of the wilds of America, we their descendants feel ourselves entitled to participate in the blessings of her luxuriant soil, which their blood and sweat manured; and that any measure or system of measures, having a tendency to banish us from her bosom, would not only be cruel, but in direct violation of those principles, which have been the boast of this republic.[5]

Given a choice, slaves too would prefer to remain here in the world they know, but as free men and women. There is no

After the Civil War, freed slaves live together in Jacksonville, Florida. Slaves preferred to stay in America even after they had been given their freedom.

reason to believe that blacks would leave for Africa willingly or even peacefully—yet another mark against colonization and its supporters.

But the essential problem of colonization is that it will not end slavery. Abolitionists who support deportation schemes are deluding themselves if they believe that they will do any good. They will not, and they do harm in turning attention away from the real struggle: emancipation without strings attached.

1. Quoted in McKitrick, *Slavery Defended*, p. 25.

2. Quoted in Dudley, *Slavery*, p. 70.

3. John C. Calhoun, "Speech of February 1837," quoted in Dudley, *Slavery*, p. 197.

4. Child, *An Appeal in Favor of That Class of Americans Called Africans*, p. 130.

5. Quoted in Patricia McKissack and Fredrick L. McKissack, *Rebels Against Slavery: American Slave Revolts*. New York: Scholastic, 1996, p. 87.

CHAPTER 3

Slaves Fighting Slavery

"We can help ourselves, for, if we lay aside abject servility, and be determined to act like men, and not brutes—the murderers among the whites would be afraid to show their cruel heads."

Resistance to Slavery Is Justified

Nothing could be more justifiable than for slaves to rise up in revolt against their masters. Slave owners oppress their slaves; they buy and sell them as cattle, they brutalize them, they attempt to strip them of their humanity. Under such circumstances, who can criticize a slave who chooses to rebel?

As circumstances now stand, a slave can have little hope of ever tasting freedom. It would be folly to believe that the South will ever give up slavery voluntarily, and blacks would be equally foolish to trust in the Northern abolitionist for help in eliminating the institution. Northerners have at best limited say in the affairs of the South, and as proslavery thought becomes more entrenched, even that limited say is shrinking rapidly. Moreover, it is by no means clear that all white men, nor even all abolitionists, truly have the welfare of the black man at heart. Consider those who devote their energies to trying to rid the continent of blacks through colonization, against the stated wishes of most African freedmen.

"Your Solemn and Imperative Duty"

Thus, black slaves can rely only on themselves to attack the evil system called slavery. Under these circumstances, resistance to slavery is not simply justified, but in some cases may actually be called for. From a moral standpoint, it is a sin for a slave to allow a slaveholder to continually abuse and harm him. True, moral philosophy tells us to turn the other cheek; but the slave-master relationship is so unhealthy that ordinary philosophy does not apply. God did not wish slavery on anyone. He would expect his people to loosen their burden by any means possible, just as he brought the Jews out of Egypt so many years ago. In truth, as minister Henry Highland Garnet writes to slaves, "To such degradation [as slavery requires] it is sinful in the extreme for you to make voluntary submission." Instead, Garnet argues, "it is your solemn and imperative duty to use every means, both moral, intellectual and physical, that promises success."[1]

Worse, slaves who submit are at heart agreeing with their masters that they are truly less than human. Denmark Vesey died for his attempt to lead a South Carolina revolt in 1822. Though he was a free black man, he cared deeply about those who remained slaves. "You are as good as any man," he would tell slaves he met. When they responded, "We are slaves," he would shake his head. "For saying so," he replied, "you deserve to be enslaved."[2] They would remain slaves, in truth, as long as they believed themselves to be.

Submission will inevitably lead to more submission. A master who gets away with brutality once is likely to commit the same injustices again. A master who is arbitrary once will be arbitrary again, to the detriment of his slaves. It is only right that slaves should resist such treatment. Similarly, the constant bowing to authority weakens black people's self-respect. A life of submission and fear of what the master may do next is no life at all, only an existence, and a poor one at that. Only through resistance can a slave hope to live the life he ought. Therefore resistance is a positive good.

What Is Resistance?

An analogy may help make this position clearer. Resistance to slavery is nothing less than self-defense. A man who protects himself from robbery by striking the robber cannot be blamed for any injuries he may cause. In the same way, the slave is not responsible for any harm he creates, if he is motivated by a desire to end the oppressive system in which he is forced to live. The Africans kidnapped and stolen into slavery generations ago had every right to resist being captured, using force if necessary. Their descendants today have the same right of resistance. The fate is the same. The response may be the same too.

Of course, resistance need not be violent, nor even physical. "We do not tell you to murder the slaveholders," reads a newspaper editorial addressed to the slaves. "But we do advise you to refuse longer to work without pay."[3] Any blow against slavery, no matter how small, is justifiable. Any blow against slavery helps restore the humanity of the slave and brings the system closer to its end. Slaves may—indeed must—protest poor treatment, from unsuitable living conditions to excessive hours and punishment.

Such resistance can take many forms: Very slow work, the deliberate destruction of tools, or even the act of breaking one's own fingers, can achieve the desired effect of demonstrating resistance.

Violent resistance is also a possibility but it may not actually be necessary. The *threat* of violent resistance may be enough to achieve freedom. "We can help ourselves," writes David Walker, a free black pamphleteer, "for, if we lay aside abject servility, and be determined to act like men, and not brutes— the murderers among the whites would be afraid to show their cruel heads." Perhaps whites would respond with further violence, but perhaps not. "Why is it," Walker asks, "that those few weak, good-for-nothing whites, are able to keep so many able men . . . in wretchedness and misery?"[4] A show of resistance, perhaps including force—a constant, continued effort across the South—might well end slavery.

Death or Slavery?

And if it did not? Let us consider the worst that might happen to a slave who revolts. Like Nat Turner in Virginia or

Nat Turner is captured after leading the 1831 Southampton insurrection, the best known and most violent slave rebellion in the United States. Turner and five other slaves killed Turner's master and his family, then proceeded to other households, killing a total of sixty whites.

Denmark Vesey's followers in South Carolina, he might be put to death. There are worse fates. A Louisiana slave chose resistance one day rather than suffer a beating. "I am not going to be whipped by anybody,"[5] he said. He was not whipped, but was shot to death instead—a choice he freely made when he decided that his dignity and worth would not permit punishment. Self-respect has value—perhaps more value than life itself. "You had far better all die—*die immediately*," Henry Garnet advises slaves, "than live slaves and entail your wretchedness upon your posterity. . . . You cannot suffer greater cruelties than you have already. *Rather die freemen than live to be the slaves.*"[6]

Slavery stands against every rule of morality and every standard of fairness. It is no wonder that slaves may choose to resist.

If all slaves chose to stage a general strike, some would surely be hurt. Others might well die. Yet there still might be great good from such a strike, for it could at last end the evil system of slavery. And if more physical resistance is called for, then let it be so. The result could be a gaining of black self-respect, and perhaps even the end of slavery itself. As Garnet writes about rebellion, "Let every slave throughout the land do this, and the hours of slavery are numbered."[7]

1. Henry Highland Garnet, *A Memorial Discourse*, quoted in Dudley, *Slavery*, p. 131.

2. Quoted in McKissack and McKissack, *Rebels Against Slavery*, p. 73.

3. "A Call to Rebellion," quoted in Dudley, *Slavery*, p. 132.

4. David Walker, *Appeal*, quoted in Dudley, *Slavery*, p. 129.

5. Quoted in Mullin, *American Negro Slavery*, p. 246.

6. Quoted in Dudley, *Slavery*, pp. 133, 135.

7. Quoted in Dudley, *Slavery*, p. 135.

"We live so little time in this world, that it is no matter how wretched or miserable we are, if it prepares us for heaven. What is forty, fifty, or sixty years, when compared to eternity."

Resistance to Slavery Is Not Justified

Slavery may be a great evil, and its elimination may be a noble goal, but not all means of doing away with slavery are acceptable. The ends do not always justify the means. Resistance on the part of the slaves, whether peaceful or violent, has no place in the movement to abolish slavery. Slave revolts of any kind are neither appropriate nor helpful.

Certainly slaves are often beaten and brutalized, but that fact in itself is not enough to justify revolt. Nor, for that matter, is the fact of the black man's status as a slave. "The slave has a right to liberty," writes minister William Ellery Channing, "but a right does not imply that it may be asserted by any and every means." The slave has a responsibility to help his master, not to destroy him. Channing continues:

> Were I confined unjustly to a house, I should have no right to free myself by setting it on fire, if thereby a family should be destroyed. An impressed seaman [a sailor kidnapped and forced into service] cannot innocently withhold his service in a storm, and would be bound to work even in ordinary weather, if this were needed to save the ship from foundering.[1]

In the same way, a slave cannot morally withhold his services from the master, no matter how badly he is treated or how unfair his bondage may be. The slave benefits from his work, after all, by receiving food and shelter from his master.

The slave also has no right to harm others or destroy property, even to free himself, for even so simple a matter as breaking a plow affects more than the slave. Destruction of property impacts the master's ability to earn his living. As such it is morally indefensible. Worse is the possibility that truly innocent people may suffer: the children of the master, who rely on him to feed them, or the buyer of the cotton, who must also support his family. Where violence is concerned there is no question about what is right and what is wrong. Two wrongs do not make a right; it is not appropriate for slaves to respond to injustice or violence with unjust or violent actions of their own.

Religion

Resistance is opposed to God's law, too. As the apostle Paul writes in Ephesians 6:5, "Servants be obedient to them that are your masters." True, slavery is brutal, and no one should be forced to labor without pay. However, God would not wish that slaves do anything other than what they are told to do. "Whatever thing a man doeth," Paul continues in Ephesians 6:8, "the same shall he receive of the Lord, whether he be bond or free." A slave is a slave until it pleases his master to set him free, or until he is set free by other means. That is his lot in life, and God would wish him to be the best slave he can be.

For indeed, the afterlife should in any case be the slaves' main concern. "We live so little time in this world," argues the slave Jupiter Hammon, "that it is no matter how wretched or miserable we are, if it prepares us for heaven. What is forty, fifty, or sixty years, when compared to eternity."[2] A slave who is resistant, who steals, lies, or harms others, will most certainly be punished by God in the next life. Slaves who rebel will remain enslaved for all time; for breaking the laws of God and his commandments, their souls will come at last to rest in hell.

A slave should be content with his lot. Indeed, God has much to offer those slaves who accept their lowly station. They, too, are part of God's plan. Remember that Christ did not minister so much to the rich and powerful as to the poor and lowly. We read in the Bible that it is easier for a camel to go through the eye of a needle than for a rich man to enter the kingdom of heaven. Since misery is likely to be the ignorant slave's fate in this life, why should he add to the misery by resisting and risking damnation? Better he should do what he is told to do, submit to his master's authority, and prepare himself for his eternal reward. As Hammon puts it, "Think of your bondage to sin and [S]atan."[3] That prospective bondage is far more important than any bondage in this world. A slave must not ruin the chance to go to heaven by disobedience here on earth.

Two slave families often lived together in one-room log cabins. These huts were poorly constructed, overcrowded, and impossible to clean.

The Effect of Resistance

It is also well to consider the effect of slave resistance. In truth, it accomplishes little, and its effects are mostly bad. Minor slave resistance is not likely to do more than annoy the master. A slave who refuses to work is apt to be beaten, and his master is apt to use him as an example of the idleness of slaves. A slave who steals from his master will be caught and whipped. This result can in no way benefit that slave or any others.

Violent resistance is even worse. Slave revolts may achieve an immediate goal—killing a few whites—but they are doomed to fail. They will result in the deaths of the leaders. In this way, slave revolt is nothing more than suicide. Rebellions such as those occurring in Virginia and South Carolina provide good examples. Denmark Vesey plotted to raid arsenals for weapons to attack and kill the whites of Charleston, South Carolina. But before he could get under-way, a fellow conspirator revealed the plan. Vesey was arrested and hanged. What value was there in his death? In Virginia, Nat Turner led an uprising that resulted in the deaths of about sixty whites on his and neighboring plantations. Along with many of his followers, Turner was executed. If slave revolts had any chance of succeeding, it might be possible to argue that they were justified. As they have no such chance, they are merely wasted effort.

Backlash

Indeed, slave revolts have actually hurt the cause of abolition. Theft, work stoppages, and violent resistance play into the masters' hands. The slave owners and their sympathizers can argue that Africans are by nature wicked and uncivilized. They can then justify all kinds of brutalities in the name of keeping the peace. "I'm nearly worried to death with [my slaves]," writes a slaveholder who had to deal with rebellious Africans. "If I had a jail, I should lock them up every night."[4] The best course of action is not to resist, not to argue, but to do the best job possible.

And in fact slave revolts often end by injuring innocent blacks. After the Turner rebellion, for example, whites rampaged through the countryside, terrorizing and killing any blacks in their path, whether they were involved in the rebellion or not. "Every day for a fortnight," writes Harriet Jacobs, a slave who lived in fear of these mobs, "I saw horsemen with some poor panting [N]egro tied to their saddles, and compelled by the lash to keep up with their speed, till they arrived at the jail yard."[5] The slaves in no way benefited from Turner's actions. Turner died, as did all his conspirators, and many innocent slaves died or were tortured as well.

It is not sensible, then, to call for slave revolt, or to support those that occur. Evil as the system of slavery may be, the proposed "cure" is worse. Revolts are ineffective. They provide opportunities for proslavery thinkers to justify slavery all the more. And in the end, rebellion of any kind is immoral; revolt jeopardizes a slave's relationship with God and violates God's laws. Revolt will not lead to a better life, either here or in the next world. Revolt, in short, is never justified.

1. William Ellery Channing, *The Duty of the Free States*, quoted in Dudley, *Slavery*, p. 123.

2. Jupiter Hammon, *An Address to the Negroes of the State of New York*, quoted in Dudley, *Slavery*, p. 126.

3. Quoted in Dudley, *Slavery*, p. 126.

4. Quoted in McKissack and McKissack, *Rebels Against Slavery*, p. 17.

5. Harriet A. Jacobs, *Incidents in the Life of a Slave Girl*, quoted in Dudley, *Slavery*, p. 150.

CHAPTER 4

Slavery and the Civil War

"The rebellion, if crushed out tomorrow, would be renewed within a year if slavery were left in full vigor."

The Goal of the Civil War Should Be the Elimination of Slavery

In the years preceding the Civil War, many controversies have arisen between North and South. Sectional differences and disagreements have helped drive a wedge between the two regions. The North is increasingly industrialized; the South, only slightly so. The North is a land of many immigrants; not so the South. Northerners and Southerners have taken varying stands on tariffs, on the advisability of war with Mexico, on the location of stagecoach and railroad routes to California, and on many other issues, both small and large. But by far the largest issue—and the one that creates the most divisiveness—is slavery.

Slavery as the Root of Dissension

Indeed, the question of slavery has divided Americans as no other issue ever has. The regions are moving in completely different directions on the topic. As Northern states have banned slavery, one by one, Southern states have affirmed the institution and made it a vital part of their economies and ways of life. Questions such as whether slavery shall be allowed in the territories, and whether Northerners are bound to return runaway slaves, have heightened the tension. It is increasingly impossible for there to be reasoned debate on slavery. Southerners see any attempt to question slavery, no matter how small, as a direct attack on the South itself. Many Northerners are weary of living in a nation where a small number of slave owners seem to hold sway, dictating what may and may not be discussed.

Several institutions, including political parties and churches, have already split apart over the question of whether to accept or reject slavery. Given this reality, it is perhaps not surprising that the Union itself has now come apart over the slavery question. As newspaper editor Horace Greeley writes, "Slavery is everywhere the inciting cause and sustaining base of treason."[1] Because slavery has driven apart the two sections of the country, it must be abolished before the nation can ever become whole again. To attempt to mend the country without attacking the root of the problem would be folly indeed.

To Save the Nation's Soul

There is a moral component to this question as well. If war is to be waged, if millions are to die, then let it be over saving the nation's soul. Slavery is an immoral institution, which permits mothers and children to be sold away from each other, which allows masters to brutalize their slaves, which sees black men and women as nothing more than property. Fighting a war to "save the Union," as some argue the North ought to do, does not justify the certain death of many thousands of soldiers. The Union is a wonderful concept, but men ought not to have to die to re-create a Union that still supports the evil of slavery. No; if men are to die, they should die attacking the great evil of our nation: the institution of slavery itself.

Morality should be reason enough to put this war on the footing of abolishing slavery. There are also practical reasons for this course of action, however. To frame the war in terms of slavery is to take the moral high ground. It puts the North on the side of right and all that is good. Consider how the issue of slavery might affect England and France, two European powers that share many interests with the South and have made no secret of their support of the Confederacy. As far as these countries are concerned, secession by the Southern states is legitimate. The Confederates "have made a nation,"[2] says British chancellor William Gladstone. To date Britain and France have maintained an official neutrality, but that may change; the South has actively sought the military intervention of both nations. Intervention such as this would seriously hurt the cause of the North; it might even turn a potential Northern victory into defeat.

But these two great nations have a history of abhorrence of slavery. Neither permits slaves in its own boundaries or in its colonies; indeed, both powers have taken the lead on abolition. Politically speaking, it would be difficult for them to lend military aid to the South if the North frames the conflict as a war against slavery. The community of civilized nations would find support of the Confederacy very hard to accept. On the other hand, if the North were waging war merely to force the South back into a Union against its will, intervention on the side of the South would be not only possible but likely.

There is also a second, perhaps even more pressing, reason to proclaim abolition as the goal of the war. Currently the North includes many false patriots: men who express loyalty to the Union but who do not have its interests at heart. Many, though not all, of these live in Missouri, Delaware, Kentucky, and Maryland, where slavery is still permitted. These states, while strategically important to the Northern cause, are also home to the most virulent antiwar and anti-Union people anywhere. To leave slavery alone there adds to the possibility of even further conflict. "Whatever strengthens or fortifies slavery in the border states," writes Greeley, "strengthens also treason and drives home the wedge intended to divide the Union."[3] Defining the war as a battle against slavery may make these traitors move farther south. If so, that would be a

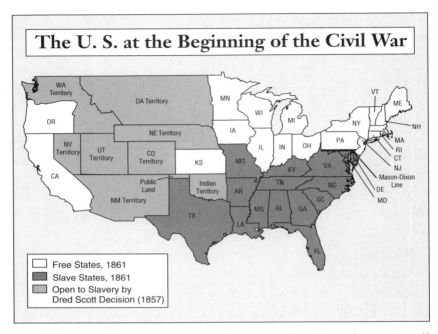

The U. S. at the Beginning of the Civil War

☐ Free States, 1861
■ Slave States, 1861
■ Open to Slavery by
Dred Scott Decision (1857)

good thing. The Union must take a stand against slavery in all
its forms and in all its homes.

". . . Or Become Slaves Themselves"

Any war waged between North and South must have as its primary goal the emancipation of all slaves and an end to slavery.
To argue for anything less ignores the root cause of the terrible
rift between North and South. A war that brings the slave states
back into the Union without addressing slavery will solve nothing. Worse, restoring the Union without abolishing slavery will
effectively mean a Confederate victory. Even if the South is
soundly defeated on the battlefield, a re-creation of the Union
without the abolition of slavery will negate that victory. The
slave states will henceforth be in a position to cut off debate
over slavery throughout the nation, reminding Northerners
that they had their chance to abolish slavery and passed it up.
Northerners will have no choice but to keep their mouths shut
over slavery. "The north," writes General Henry Halleck,
"must either destroy the slave-oligarchy [government], or
become slaves themselves."[4]

And if the North does not choose to keep silent in a restored Union with slavery permitted? Then war is bound to be repeated. The issue of slavery separates the sections of the country more than any other. If that issue goes unresolved now, it will appear again. "The rebellion, if crushed out tomorrow," writes Greeley, "would be renewed within a year if slavery were left in full vigor."[5] Our best hope to avoid further conflict is to eliminate slavery now. And the best way of doing that is to make abolition the primary aim of the Civil War.

1. Horace Greeley, *New York Tribune*, August 19, 1862, quoted in Dudley, *Slavery*, p. 261.

2. Quoted in Bruce Catton, *The Civil War*. Boston: Houghton Mifflin, 1960, p. 104.

3. Quoted in Dudley, *Slavery*, p. 262.

4. H.W. Halleck to U.S. Grant, March 31, 1863, quoted in Berlin et al., *Free at Last*, p. 103.

5. Quoted in Dudley, *Slavery*, p. 264.

"It would be foolish to believe that emancipation will settle all differences between North and South. What matters most is the Union. Without reestablishing the Union, everything else is lost. That must be the ultimate goal of the war."

Elimination of Slavery Should Not Be the Goal of the Civil War

There is no tragedy greater than war, and there is no war more tragic than a war between brothers. This is what Americans face in the current war now being waged, the war between North and South. Many issues divide the two sections; many issues have torn the nation into pieces. Certainly slavery is one such issue, but it is far from the only source of difference, mistrust, and anger.

The roots of the conflict, indeed, lie in much more than slavery. The two regions of the country have developed different ways of life, ways of life that are distinct and often at odds with each other. Whereas one section benefits from tariffs on goods imported into the nation, the other section is harmed by tariffs. And yet the same law must apply to all states. Whereas New Englanders disapproved of the war with Mexico, most Southerners enthusiastically accepted it. Debates on many subjects, from internal improvements to education, have often pitted North against South. The facts do not support the contention that slavery is all that divides the two regions.

These quarrels must be resolved if the Union is to be restored. A restored Union must be less divisive and angry than it has been heretofore. And certainly the question of slavery must be resolved as well. But it may not be permitted to take precedence over all else. It would be foolish to believe that emancipation will settle all differences between North and South. What matters most is the Union. Without re-establishing the Union, everything else is lost. That must be the ultimate goal of the war.

Concerns About Emancipation

If the majority wishes to free the slaves, then the slaves should be freed. But emancipation should by no means be the primary goal of a war. War will cost thousands of lives and untold misery. And for what? For something that could be accomplished in other, more peaceful ways? Rather than put money, time, and blood into a war to abolish slavery, put the same funds and effort into working out a plan for gradual, compensated emancipation without loss of life.

Moreover, a war to force emancipation on Southerners is unwise. If emancipation is the requirement for taking the slave states back into the Union, then the result will be generations of anger and even hatred on the part of Southerners. A conquered people, forced to give up a system they hold dear, will hold a grudge. The North cannot afford to treat the South as an enemy, imposing its will on those states as though they have no identity of their own. To fight a war to end slavery is to eliminate all chance of a reunited nation with a cooperative and productive future.

Border States and Northern Men

There are further obstacles to making this war a fight against slavery. In the first place, there are many who love the Union but who do not hate slavery. Four border states allow slavery but have nevertheless remained loyal to the Union. In each there is substantial opinion that slavery is not a bad thing, indeed it may even be a positive good. Fight the war as a battle to abolish slavery and those states will likely go to the Confederacy. Without them, the balance of power would shift dramatically.

Consider the consequences. Currently the North has a decided edge in population and therefore in army size as well. This is a significant advantage, especially in a long war, but with four states removed from the Northern side and placed squarely with the Confederacy, the two armies would be much more equal in numbers. The national capital would be sandwiched between two slave-owning Confederate states, Virginia and Maryland. Most likely it would have to be abandoned, at great cost and embarrassment to the Union.

Furthermore, with its base of operations on the borders of Northern states such as Ohio, Illinois, and Pennsylvania, the Confederacy could launch assaults into Northern territory far more easily. Far from being able to push ever deeper into Southern territory, the Northern army would have to spend much of its time defending its own. The loss of the border states would be an utter disaster for the North, and a disaster that would logically follow from the idea that the war should be fought against slavery.

Worse, the announcement that abolition is the aim of the war would distress many loyal Northerners. Certainly there are many abolitionists in the North, men and women such as the Germans in Milwaukee, the old Yankees in New Hampshire, and the Quakers in Philadelphia, who hate slavery and all that it stands for. But they do not represent the thinking of all the people of the North. In the southern parts of Indiana, in much of New Jersey, in New York City, and other places, there is not much sympathy for the plight of the slave. As a soldier writes: "It is not for the emancipation of the African race that I fight. I want nothing to do with the negro. I want them as far from me as is possible to conceive."[1]

A crowd gathers as a man preaches the abolition of slavery at a public antislavery meeting.

These men may fight to preserve the Union. They may be willing to die to preserve it. They have turned out in large numbers to join the army and support the restoration of the Union. However, they are not likely to do so in the same numbers and with the same enthusiasm if the primary goal is freeing the slave.

The End of Slavery

And why should they? Slaves are not ready yet for emancipation. There is no plan in place for what to do with them after the war is over. Even those white abolitionists entrusted with the job of educating the newly freed slaves admit that blacks will not be ready for many years to take their place in society. "Though it is not their fault that they have been kept brutally ignorant," writes Lydia Maria Child, "it unfits them for voters."[2] It is not as though Africans will be qualified to rebuild the South after the war, even though the war was fought to free them.

Indeed, Northerners have reason to be particularly worried about the possibility of sudden emancipation. Former slaves

President Lincoln and his advisers gather during the signing of the Emancipation Proclamation—the historic document that declared Confederate slaves free.

will likely flood the North after abolition comes, depressing wages and making it hard for laborers to obtain work. They will displace the Northerners who are already there. "Our soldiers," writes an Ohio congressman, "when they return, one hundred thousand strong, to their Ohio homes, will find these negroes . . . filling their places, felling timber, plowing ground, gathering crops, &c." Landowners and businessmen of the North will suffer, too. "When work grows irksome [for former slaves]," the congressman warns, "and they become too lazy to work, they will steal."[3] It is therefore hard to condemn the Northerners who would lay down their arms if they were told the war was not about restoring the Union, but instead about freeing the slaves.

The Union must be saved. Nothing else matters. "What I do about slavery and the colored race I do because I believe it helps the Union," writes President Abraham Lincoln, "and what I forbear I forbear because I do *not* believe it would help to save the Union."[4] Lincoln's focus is on the Union, not on slavery. "If I could save the Union without freeing *any* slave," he writes, "I would do it; and if I could save it by freeing *all* the slaves, I would do it; and if I could do it by freeing some and leaving others alone, I would also do that."[5] Lincoln's attitude is a proper one; may all loyal Northerners, abolitionist or not, learn from it.

1. Quoted in Timothy Levi Biel, *Life in the North During the Civil War.* San Diego: Lucent Books, 1997, p. 101.

2. Lydia Maria Child, *Anti-Slavery Catechism,* quoted in Dudley, *Slavery,* p. 206.

3. Quoted in Biel, *Life in the North During the Civil War,* p. 103.

4. Abraham Lincoln to Horace Greeley, August 22, 1862, quoted in Dudley, *Slavery,* p. 266.

5. Quoted in Dudley, *Slavery,* p. 266.

APPENDIX

Excerpts from Original Documents Pertaining to Slavery

Document 1: Slaves Likened to Colonists

An argument often made by antislavery advocates was that America was founded on the assumption that all men were created equal. This argument had its earliest foundation in the years leading up to the Revolution. James Otis was one of many colonists who argued that the treatment of the colonists by the British was similar to the treatment of slaves by their masters. Both, he concluded, were equally wrong and immoral.

The colonists are by the law of nature freeborn, as indeed all men are, white or black. . . . Does it follow that 'tis right to enslave a man because he is black? Will short curled hair like wool instead of Christian hair, as 'tis called by those whose hearts are as hard as the nether millstone, help the argument? Can any logical inference in favor of slavery be drawn from a flat nose, a long or short face? Nothing better can be said in favor of a trade that is the most shocking violation of the law of nature, has a direct tendency to diminish the idea of the inestimable value of liberty, and makes every dealer in it a tyrant, from the director of an African [slave-trading] company to the petty chapman in needles and pins on the unhappy coast. It is a clear truth that those who every day barter away other men's liberty will soon care little for their own.

James Otis, from the pamphlet *The Rights of the British Colonies Asserted and Proved*, 1764, quoted in William Dudley, ed., *Slavery*. San Diego: Greenhaven Press, 1992, p. 52.

Document 2: Liberty Must Be Earned

One of the most common proslavery arguments held that Africans were not in any sense equal to whites. South Carolina senator John Calhoun was one of the leading proponents of this position.

It is a great and dangerous error to suppose that all people are equally entitled to liberty. It is a reward to be earned, not a blessing to be gratuitously lavished on all alike;—a reward reserved for the intelligent, the patriotic, the virtuous and deserving;—and not a boon to be bestowed on a people too ignorant, degraded and vicious, to be capable either of appreciating or of enjoying it. . . . The progress of a people rising from a lower to a higher point in the scale of liberty, is necessarily slow;—and by attempting to precipitate, we either retard, or permanently defeat it.

John C. Calhoun, *Disquisition on Government*, published 1854, quoted in Eric McKitrick, ed., *Slavery Defended: The Views of the Old South*. Englewood Cliffs, NJ: Prentice-Hall, 1963, p. 9.

Document 3: What the Bible Has to Say

The question of what religion had to say about slavery stirred high passions on both sides. Typically Southerners quoted Bible verses to illustrate the moral rightness of slavery, while Northerners looked behind the verses themselves for the spirit in which they were intended. This excerpt from Lydia Maria Child's work encapsulates the Northern argument.

Among other apologies for slavery, it has been asserted that the Bible does not forbid it. Neither does it forbid the counterfeiting of a bank-bill. It is the *spirit* of the Holy Word, not its particular *expressions*, which must be a rule for our conduct. How can slavery be reconciled with the maxim, "Do unto others, as ye would that others should do unto you?" Does not the command, "Thou shalt not *steal*," prohibit *kidnapping*? And how does whipping men to death agree with the injunction, "Thou shalt do no *murder*?" Are we not told "to loose the bands of wickedness, to undo the heavy burdens, to let the oppressed go free, and to break every yoke?". . . Modern slavery is so unlike Hebrew servitude, and its regulations are so diametrically opposed to the rules of the Gospel, which came to bring deliverance to the captive, that it is idle to dwell upon this point.

Lydia Maria Child, *An Appeal in Favor of That Class of Americans Called Africans.* 1836. Reprinted New York: Arno Press, 1968, p. 32.

Document 4: Slavery as a Positive Force

As the nineteenth century progressed, some Southern thinkers began to take the offensive in debates about slavery. Where many colonial slave owners had admitted that slavery made them uncomfortable, later thinkers admitted no such thing. Southerners began to contrast the treatment of working-class Northerners and Europeans with the conditions of slavery. In the minds of men such as George Fitzhugh, there was no comparison.

There is no rivalry, no competition to get employment among slaves, as among free laborers. Nor is there a war between master and slave. The master's interest prevents his reducing the slave's allowance or wages in infancy or sickness, for he might lose the slave by so doing. His feeling for his slave never permits him to stint him in old age. The slaves are all well fed, well clad, have plenty of fuel, and are happy. They have no dread of the future—no fear of want. . . . The slaveholder is like other men; he will not tread on the worm nor break the bruised reed. The ready submission of the slave, nine times out of ten, disarms his wrath even when the slave has offended. . . . We go farther, and say the slaveholder is better than others—because he has greater occasion for the exercise of the affections. His whole life is spent in providing for the minutest wants of others, in taking care of them in sickness and in health. Hence he is the least selfish of men.

George Fitzhugh, *Sociology for the South, or the Failure of Free Society.* Richmond, VA: A. Morris, 1854, pp. 246–48.

Document 5: Slavery as Brutality

Many narratives from former slaves have been collected, some while slavery was still going on, others as much as seventy-five or eighty years later. Antislavery supporters often published the most inhumane descriptions of treatment as a way of opening people's eyes to the horrors of the system. This excerpt is a slave's recollection of life on a Southern plantation.

My master used to throw me in a buck [a particular position] and whip me. He would put my hands together and tie them. Then he would strip me naked. Then would make me squat down. Then he would run a stick through behind my knees and in front of my elbows. My knee was up against my chest. My hands was tied together just in front of my shins. The stick between my arms and my knees held me in a squat. That's what they call a buck. You couldn't stand up and you couldn't get your feet out. You couldn't do nothing but just squat there and take what he put on. You couldn't move no way at all. . . . He would whip me on one side till that was sore and full of blood and then he would whip me on the other side till that was all tore up.

Ella Wilson, former slave, quoted in Julius Lester, *To Be a Slave.* New York: Dial Press, 1968, pp. 36-37.

Document 6: Immediate Abolition

The abolition movement began slowly in the United States, but by the 1830s it was in full swing, especially in New England, Philadelphia, and parts of the Midwest. Increasingly abolitionists attacked slavery on all fronts: It was immoral, it was brutal, it was economically unsound. The American Anti-Slavery Society was among the most uncompromising abolitionist organizations in the North. As the following excerpt makes clear, its members fought not only slavery but also deportation and racial prejudice. These were instructions to Theodore Weld, the group's leader.

You will inculcate every where, the great fundamental principle of IMMEDIATE ABOLITION, as the duty of all masters, on the ground that slavery is both unjust and unprofitable. . . . We reprobate the idea of compensation to slave holders, because it implies the right of slavery. It is also unnecessary, because the abolition of slavery will be an advantage, as free labor is found to be more profitable than the labor of slaves. We also reprobate all plans of expatriation, by whatever specious pretences covered, as a remedy for slavery, for they all proceed from prejudices against color; and we hold that the duty of the whites in regard to this cruel prejudice is not to indulge it, but to repent and overcome it.

American Anti-Slavery Society, "Instructions to Theodore Weld," 1834, quoted in John L. Thomas, *Slavery Attacked: The Abolitionist Crusade.* Englewood Cliffs, NJ: Prentice-Hall, 1965, p. 25.

Document 7: The Case for Colonization

While colonization was mainly meant to rid the United States of free blacks, many of its supporters hoped to send slaves back to Africa as well. Colonization advocates defended their plans partly on the basis that racial prejudice prevented Africans from ever being able to take part in American society.

The managers [of the American Colonization Society] consider it clear that causes exist and are operating to prevent [blacks'] improvement and elevation to any considerable extent as a class, in this country, which are fixed, not only beyond the control of the friends of humanity, but of any human power. Christianity will not do for them here, what it will do for them in Africa. This is not the fault of the colored man, nor Christianity but an ordination of Providence, and no more to be changed than the laws of Nature!

Last Annual Report of American Colonization Society, quoted in Lydia Maria Child, *An Appeal in Favor of That Class of Americans Called Africans.* 1836. Reprinted New York: Arno Press, 1968, pp. 133–34.

Document 8: For Gradual Emancipation

Especially after the Revolution, many people presented plans for freeing the slaves. Most supported some kind of gradual emancipation program, as the plan presented here by Virginia planter Ferdinando Fairfax demonstrates.

It seems to be the general opinion, that emancipation must be gradual; since, to deprive a man, at once, of all his right in the property of his negroes, would be the height of injustice, and such as, in this country, would never be submitted to: and the resources of government are by no means adequate to making at once a full compensation. It must therefore be by voluntary consent—consequently in a gradual manner.

Ferdinando Fairfax, *Plan for Liberating the Negroes Within the United States,* 1790, quoted in William Dudley, ed., *Slavery.* San Diego: Greenhaven Press, 1992, p. 166.

Document 9: Fear of Africans

Colonization forces played on Americans' generosity in giving Africans a better life back home in Africa. When this appeal failed, they were not above using scare tactics as well, as this excerpt shows.

[Colonization] tends, and may powerfully tend, to rid us, gradually and entirely, in the United States, of slaves and slavery: a great moral and political evil, of increasing virulence and extent, from which much mischief is now felt, and very great calamity in future is justly apprehended. . . . The alarming danger of cherishing in our bosom a distinct nation, which can never become incorporated with us, while it rapidly increases in numbers and improves in intelligence; learning from us the arts of peace and war, the secret of its own strength, and the talent of combining and directing its force—a nation which must ever be hostile to us, from feeling and interest, because it can never incorporate with us, nor participate in the advantages which we enjoy; the danger of such a nation in our bosom need not be pointed out to any reflecting mind.

Robert Goodloe Harper, in *First Annual Report,* American Colonization Society, 1817, quoted in William Dudley, ed., *Slavery.* San Diego: Greenhaven Press, 1992, pp. 184–85.

Document 10: Against Colonization

The staunchest abolitionists, such as Theodore Weld, Lydia Maria Child, and William Lloyd Garrison, rejected the notion of colonization for various reasons. In this excerpt, Garrison dismisses the notion that colonization could ever do what its supporters wanted.

What has the [American Colonization] Society accomplished? Much, unquestionably, for a single association, engaged in a hazardous enterprise, and supported by the uncertain charities of the public. But has it, in any degree, sustained its high pretensions? . . . or made any visible impression upon the growth of slavery? Assuredly not. It has been in existence about thirteen years—a term amply sufficient to test its capacity and usefulness. Its annual transportation to Liberia, I believe, has averaged *one hundred* souls. During the same period, the *increase* of the colored population has amounted to upwards of *five hundred thousand.* And yet such is the colonization mania . . . that no demonstration of its inefficiency, however palpable, can shake the faith of its advocates.

William Lloyd Garrison, "Henry Clay's Colonization Address," March 5, 1830, quoted in John Thomas, *Slavery Attacked: The Abolitionist Crusade.* Englewood Cliffs, NJ: Prentice-Hall, 1965, p. 9.

Document 11: Rise and Revolt!

Slave revolts were an ever-present threat for Southerners, especially those who lived on isolated plantations where blacks greatly outnumbered whites. Although nearly all weapons were in the hands of the white people, many whites and black abolitionists urged slaves to rise up and revolt. This document, written by a preacher who was a former slave, details some of the reasons why.

Brethren, arise, arise! Strike for your lives and liberties. Now is the day and the hour. . . . It is in your power so to torment the God-cursed slave-holders that they will be glad to let you go free. If the scale was turned, and black men were the masters and white men the slaves, every destructive agent and element would be employed to lay the oppressor low. Danger and death would hang over their heads day and night. Yes, the tyrants would meet with plagues more terrible than those of Pharaoh. But you are a patient people. You act as though you were made for the special use of these devils. You act as though your daughters were born to pamper the lusts of your masters and overseers. . . . In the name of God, we ask, are you men? Where is the blood of your fathers? Has it all run out of your veins? Awake, awake; millions of voices are calling you! Your dead fathers speak to you from their graves. Heaven, as with a voice of thunder, calls on you to arise from the dust.

Henry Highland Garnet, "An Address to the Slaves of the United States of America," 1843, quoted in John Thomas, *Slavery Attacked: The Abolitionist Crusade.* Englewood Cliffs, NJ: Prentice-Hall, 1965, pp. 103–104.

Document 12: Vesey's Rebellion

Before Nat Turner's rebellion, Denmark Vesey's was the best known in the South. In 1822, Vesey plotted to raid the garrisons of Charleston, South Carolina, and take over the city with the help of free blacks like himself and slaves. His plot was uncovered before it could be put into action, however, and Vesey was put to death. This excerpt comes from the testimony of one of Vesey's followers.

[Vesey asked a slave named Bacchus] seven queries such as Did His master u[se] him well—Yes he believed so. Did He eat the same as his master, Yes sometimes not always as well as his master. Did his master not sleep on a soft bed, Yes. Did he Bacchus sleep on as soft a bed as his master. No. Who made his master. God. Who made you. God. And then ar[e]n't you as good as your master if God made him and you, ar[e]n't you as free, Yes. Then why don't you join and fight your master. Does your master use you well. Yes, I believe so. Does he whip you when you do wrong, Yes sometimes. Then why don't [yo]u as you are as free as your master, turn about and fight for yourself.

Confessions of Bacchus, the slave of Mr. Hammet, 1822, quoted in Michael Mullin, ed., *American Negro Slavery: A Documentary History*. New York: Harper and Row, 1976, pp. 230–31.

Document 13: Rebellion Is Not Justified

Jupiter Hammon was a slave who believed that rebellion was unjustified. His was the first writing by a black person to be published in America. Hammon's perspective was that freedom would come through religion rather than through disobedience.

We have no right to stay when we are sent on errands, any longer than to do the business we were sent upon. All the time spent idly, is spent wickedly, and is unfaithfulness to our masters. In these things I must say, that I think many of you are guilty. I know that many of you endeavor to excuse yourselves, and say, that you are under great temptations to be unfaithful and take from your masters. But this will not do, God will certainly punish you for stealing and for being unfaithful. All that we have to mind is our own duty. If God has put us in bad circumstances, that is not our fault, and he will not punish us for it. If any are wicked in keeping us so, we cannot help it, they must answer to God for it. Nothing will serve as an excuse to us for not doing our duty. The same God will judge both them and us.

Jupiter Hammon, *An Address to the Negroes of the State of New York*, 1786, quoted in William Dudley, ed., *Slavery*. San Diego: Greenhaven Press, 1992, p. 123.

Document 14: Slaves Taking Advantage

It was an article of faith among many Southerners that slavery was more trouble than it was worth. Slave owners often believed that slaves shirked work and that owners had no recourse. This excerpt, from the years just before the Civil War, details that belief.

"The women on a plantation," said one extensive Virginian slave owner to me, "will hardly earn their salt, after they come to the breeding age: they don't come to the field and you go to the quarters and ask the old nurse what's the matter and she says, 'Oh, she's not well, Master; she's not fit to work, sir'; and what can you do? You have to take her word for it that something or other is the matter with her; and you dare not set her to work; and so she lays up till she feels like taking the air again, and plays the lady at your expense."

Frederick Law Olmsted, *Journey in the Seaboard Slave States*, 1856, quoted in Julius Lester, *To Be a Slave*. New York: Dial Press, 1968, p. 100.

Document 15: Arbitrary Power

Treatment of slaves was all the more horrible because brutality could happen at any time and for any reason, as this document makes clear.

One Saturday morning little Missy [the slavemaster's daughter] was sleeping late. She did not have to go to school. Ol' Missy told me to go and make up her bed. I went in and she didn't want to get up so that I could make the bed. I told her then that it was late and that ol' Missy said for her to get up. Then she got mad, jumped up in the bed and said, "You black dog, get out of here. I'll get up when I get ready." With that she slapped me as hard as she could right in my face. I saw stars. As soon as I got back to myself, I swung at her and if she hadn't been so quick I would have almost killed her for I hit at her with my fist and with all the force I had. I was just about ready to jump up on the bed and choke the life out of her when ol' Missy happened in.

Anonymous slave, quoted in Julius Lester, *To Be a Slave*. New York: Dial Press, 1968, pp. 127–28.

Document 16: Saving the Union

As president, Abraham Lincoln walked a tight line between two factions: those who felt that he should be more actively engaged in fighting slavery, and those who had qualms about waging war to begin with. In this letter to newspaper editor Horace Greeley, Lincoln explains his actions and his reasoning behind them.

I would save the Union. I would save it the shortest way under the Constitution. The sooner the national authority can be restored, the nearer Union will be "the Union as it was." If there be those who would not save the Union unless they could at the same time *save* slavery, I do not agree with them. If there be those who would not save the Union unless they could at the same time *destroy* slavery, I do not agree with them. My paramount object in this struggle *is* to save the Union, and is *not* either to save or destroy slavery. If I could save the Union without freeing *any* slave, I would do it; and if I could save it by freeing *all* the slaves, I would do it; and if I could do it by freeing some and leaving others alone, I would also do that. What I do about slavery and the colored race I do because I believe it helps to save this Union; and what I forbear I forbear because I do *not* believe it would help to save the Union.

Abraham Lincoln, letter of August 22, 1862, quoted in William Dudley, ed., *Slavery*. San Diego: Greenhaven Press, 1992, p. 266.

Document 17: Slave Owners Are Coddled

Horace Greeley, editor of a New York City newspaper, was among those who felt that Lincoln's policy was not sufficiently aggressive in going after slavery. In a letter to Lincoln written early in the Civil War, he detailed some of the ways in which slave owners were being coddled by administration policies. Greeley was particularly upset about the treatment of runaway slaves, who often were returned to their masters.

We complain that the officers of your armies have habitually repelled rather than invited the approach of slaves who would have gladly taken the risks of escaping from their Rebel masters to our camps, bringing intelligence often of inestimable value to the Union cause. We complain that those who *have* thus escaped to us, avowing a willingness to do for us whatever might be required, have been brutally and madly repulsed, and often surrendered to be scourged, maimed, and tortured by the ruffian traitors who pretend to own them. We complain that a large proportion of our regular Army officers, with many of the volunteers, evince far more solicitude to uphold slavery than to put down the rebellion.

Horace Greeley, *New York Tribune*, 1862, quoted in William Dudley, ed., *Slavery*, San Diego: Greenhaven Press, 1992, p. 263.

Document 18: Slavery and Truth

Many abolitionist Northerners were thrilled with Lincoln's election in 1860. As this excerpt makes clear, abolitionists believed that slave power had run the nation for most of its history and that the election of Lincoln on a platform including the opposition of slavery was exactly what the nation needed—whether abolition was the primary aim of the war or not.

Slavery has always ruled this country. As soon as a seat of power was reared, Slavery assumed it. . . . It ruled commerce, it expunged the truth of history . . . it clasped the Bible with handcuffs and festooned the Cross of Christ with chains. . . . It was the noblest revolution the world ever saw that placed Abraham Lincoln in the White House at Washington; the noblest, because the first ever known upon this planet where the legitimate weapons of Truth were alone used. These mighty strongholds yielded to the voices, the persuasions, the reasons, of earnest and just men; they were besieged with arrows of light, shelled with the bombs of Free School and Free Thought.

Moncure Conway, *The Rejected Stone*, 1861, quoted in John Thomas, *Slavery Attacked: The Abolitionist Crusade*. Englewood Cliffs, NJ: Prentice-Hall, 1965, p. 170.

Document 19: Unfairness

The population of the four border states—Delaware, Maryland, Kentucky, and Missouri—was of critical importance to both sides in the Civil War. These four states permitted slavery, but in none of them was slavery as common as in most other Southern states. Residents of these states were often happy to join the war to help preserve the Union, but were rarely so happy to find themselves fighting slavery, as this letter to Abraham Lincoln from a slave-owning Kentucky officer makes clear.

When I became a soldier I sacrificed a large and lucrative practice as an attorney in Philadelphia and placed my property in this state [Kentucky] at the mercy of our enemies—who have revenged themselves largely upon me—and now my utter ruin is to be Completed by our own officers to promote a fanatical partizan theory—which not only ignores gratitude as a principle; but does me and many loyal men of my state bold wrong for a supposed benefit to another race. Mr. President is this right and will you sanction it? . . . I must dissent from your policy of *freeing* the slaves of rebels, which would result in great wrong to loyal slave owners, as well as to all loyal men burthened with this immense war debt. . . . Were I Commander in Chief I would never trample upon the Constitutional rights of a loyal people in a loyal state whereby our friends would be estranged and our enemies advantaged.

Colonel Marcellus Mundy, Kentucky slaveholder and commander of a Union regiment, 1862, quoted in Ira Berlin et al., *Free at Last*. New York: New Press, 1992, p. 83.

CHRONOLOGY

1619
The first blacks arrive in what is now the United States; most likely they were indentured servants rather than slaves.

1641
Massachusetts becomes the first colony to mention slavery in its laws.

1688
Pennsylvania Quakers issue the first written condemnation of slavery in America.

1739
The Stono rebellion in South Carolina leads to the execution of twenty slaves who killed white merchants and families.

1775
The first abolition society in America is started in Philadelphia.

1776
The Declaration of Independence is signed July 4; this document asserts that "all men are created free" without specifying "white men."

1777
Vermont becomes the first of the former colonies to abolish slavery.

1784
Several Northern former colonies establish plans for gradual emancipation of their remaining slaves.

1787–1788
The Constitution is ratified; it extends the slave trade for twenty more years.

1787
The Northwest Ordinance prohibits slavery in the new territories of Illinois, Wisconsin, Michigan, Ohio, Indiana, and part of Minnesota.

1793
Toussaint Louverture leads a successful slave revolt in Haiti, overthrowing European rule.

1793
Eli Whitney's invention of the cotton gin leads to increased demand for slaves in areas that can produce cotton.

1800
The Gabriel Prosser rebellion in Virginia leads to the death of Prosser and his conspirators.

1817
The American Colonization Society is founded.

1820
The Missouri Compromise admits Missouri as a slave state and Maine as a free state; it also draws a line across the western territories at 36° 30' north latitude, north of which slavery will not be allowed.

1822
The Denmark Vesey rebellion in Charleston, South Carolina, is stopped while in the planning stages, resulting in the executions of Vesey and his followers.

1831
William Lloyd Garrison begins publication of his antislavery news-paper, *The Liberator.*

1831
The Nat Turner rebellion in Southampton County, Virginia, results in the deaths of many local whites along with Turner, all his fol-lowers, and many uninvolved slaves.

1833
The American Anti-Slavery Society is founded in Philadelphia; it urges immediate emancipation.

1836
Congress adopts a gag rule essentially stopping debate on slavery.

1850
The Compromise of 1850 admits California as a free state and also enacts a more restrictive law calling for the return of runaway slaves to their masters.

1854
The Republican Party is founded in the upper Midwest. It adopts an aggressively antislavery stance.

1854

The Kansas-Nebraska Act permits slavery in those territories that want it.

1860

Abraham Lincoln wins a four-way race for president.

1860

South Carolina secedes.

1861

The Confederacy is established.

1861

The Civil War begins.

1862

Lincoln issues his Emancipation Proclamation, which actually frees no slaves, but promises that all slaves in areas currently held by the Confederates will be set free once Union armies take charge.

1865

The Civil War ends.

1865

The Thirteenth Amendment, eliminating slavery, is ratified.

STUDY QUESTIONS

Chapter 1

1. How is racism reflected in the arguments of both abolitionists and slaveholders?

2. Compare the arguments in this chapter with current debates on one of the following: gay rights, feminism, or affirmative action. How are similar religious, moral, economic, and historical arguments used in each case?

3. Both sides claimed that they had the best interests of the slaves at heart. What other interests motivated their actions?

4. If people wished to make themselves slaves, argued proslavery thinker George Fitzhugh, they ought to be allowed to do so. How might an abolitionist respond?

Chapter 2

1. Slaveholders contended that factory workers in the North were worse off than slaves. What arguments could be made to counter that view?

2. The people arguing for immediate emancipation used certain kinds of evidence to support their points. The people arguing for gradual emancipation used evidence, too. How does that evidence differ?

3. Judging from their arguments, how do you think the people expressing Viewpoints 1 and 2 would have responded to secession? Which group would have been more likely to oppose it? Support your conclusions with evidence from the viewpoints.

Chapter 3

1. How are arguments against slave revolts similar to arguments supporting slavery in Chapter 1?

2. What assumptions about slavery are made by those who believed that slave revolts are justified? How do they reflect the arguments expressed in the first two chapters?

3. Compare the arguments regarding slave revolts with current debates about militias, abortion, or war. What uses do both sides make of moral, religious, or practical arguments?

Chapter 4

1. The two viewpoints in this chapter disagree on whether slavery was the central cause of the Civil War. What kinds of evidence do the two sides use to support their arguments?

2. Which parts of these arguments are based on morality? Which are based on practicality? Which style of argument do you find more compelling? Why?

3. Is it reasonable to oppose the extension of slavery but be unwilling to interfere with slavery itself, as Abraham Lincoln originally did? Explain why or why not.

FOR FURTHER READING

Timothy Levi Biel, *Life in the North During the Civil War.* San Diego: Lucent Books, 1997. A study of the North intended for young adults. Includes information on the reactions of white Northerners to the question of slavery and their views on abolition.

Susanne Everett, *History of Slavery.* Edison, NJ: Chartwell Books, 1976. A consideration of slavery throughout history and across the world. It includes chapters on slavery in the Middle East, in the Caribbean, and in ancient times in addition to the American South. The book is exceptionally well illustrated.

Leonard W. Ingraham, *Slavery in the United States.* New York: Franklin Watts, 1968. A short and readable history of slavery. The book gives a brief account of revolts, the slave trade, and many aspects of slave life as well as the political issues surrounding slavery.

Florence and J.B. Jackson, *The Black Man in America, 1619–1790.* New York: Franklin Watts, 1970. Well-illustrated, brief description of the lives of slaves and free blacks, women as well as men, during the colonial era and the first few years thereafter. The book has a particular emphasis on the daily life of African Americans.

Julius Lester, *To Be a Slave.* New York: Dial Press, 1968. A collection of slave reminiscences with commentary. Chapters include "The Plantation," "The Auction Block," and "Emancipation," always focusing on the actual words and recollections of slaves.

Patricia McKissack and Fredrick L. McKissack, *Rebels Against Slavery: American Slave Revolts.* New York: Scholastic, 1996. A very readable description of slave revolts from early colonial times through to the Civil War. The authors focus on the details of raids as well as on the circumstances of slavery that drove some slaves to desperation.

Michael Mullin, ed., *American Negro Slavery: A Documentary History.* New York: Harper and Row, 1976. Many documents relating to the history of slavery in the South, with a particular emphasis on slavery in colonial times; useful commentary accompanies the text.

WORKS CONSULTED

Ira Berlin et al., *Free at Last*. New York: New Press, 1992. A collection of documents relating to slavery and its role in the Civil War. Includes letters from Southern farmers, government officials, generals regarding the emancipation of slaves, and others.

John Blassingame, *The Slave Community*. New York: Oxford University Press, 1979. A general history of slavery. The book makes extensive use of slave sources to help interpret the slave system.

Margaret Stimmann Branson and Edward E. France, *The Human Side of Afro-American History*. Lexington, MA: Ginn, 1972. A sourcebook of readings on African American history. Includes information on the slave trade, the daily life of slaves, the debates on the morality of slavery, and the Civil War era.

Bruce Catton, *The Civil War*. Boston: Houghton Mifflin, 1960. A carefully researched, well-written one-volume account of the Civil War. Gives a short but thorough account of slavery during the war and its role in the breakup of the Union.

Lydia Maria Child, *An Appeal in Favor of That Class of Americans Called Africans*. 1836. Reprinted New York: Arno Press, 1968. A brief in favor of the rights of African Americans. Child's tone throughout is moderate and conciliatory, but she presents clear and forceful arguments.

William Dudley, ed., *Slavery*. San Diego: Greenhaven Press, 1992. A collection of documents with commentary illustrating many of the great controversies over slavery. Chapters include "Abolitionism and Its Opponents," "Slavery Divides a Nation," and "Slave Resistance, Slave Rebellion."

Stanley Elkins, *Slavery: A Problem in American Institutional Life*. Chicago: University of Chicago Press, 1976. Elkins's history compares slavery as an extremely brutal and harsh system to a concentration camp during World War II.

George Fitzhugh, *Sociology for the South, or the Failure of Free Society.* Richmond, VA: A. Morris, 1854. Fitzhugh was one of the staunchest defenders of the South and the Southern system of slavery. This is among the clearest single arguments in favor of slavery.

Robert Fogel and Stanley Engerman, *Time on the Cross.* New York: University Press of America, 1985. An overview of slavery, controversial because of its emphasis on quantitative analysis of slavery using numbers and statistics. Its basic thrust is that slavery was not as bad as most researchers have concluded.

Eugene Genovese, *Roll, Jordan, Roll: The World the Slaves Made.* New York: Random House, 1976. Genovese argues that Southern slaves had room for some limited freedom within the structure of the pre–Civil War plantation.

B.C. Hall and C.T. Wood, *The South.* New York: Touchstone, 1995. An exploration of the factors that make the South a distinctive region within the United States today. The authors use historical analysis and plenty of facts, including research into slavery and the Civil War, to draw their conclusions.

William Sumner Jenkins, *Pro-Slavery Thought in the Old South.* Chapel Hill: University of North Carolina Press, 1935. A study of some of the defenses of slavery advanced by Southerners before the Civil War. The author extensively quotes original writings and speeches.

Frances Anne Kemble, *Journal of a Resident on a Georgia Plantation in 1838–1839.* New York: Harper and Brothers, 1863. "Fannie" Kemble was a British actress who married a Southerner and spent an unhappy winter in Georgia on his plantation. This book explains some of her thoughts and feelings about that time.

Eric McKitrick, ed., *Slavery Defended: The Views of the Old South.* Englewood Cliffs, NJ: Prentice-Hall, 1963. A selection of documents in defense of slavery. The sources range from government officials to political economists to ordinary citizens.

Edmund Morgan, *American Slavery, American Freedom*. New York: Norton, 1975. Morgan deals primarily with the decision to bring slavery to Virginia in the 1600s and the consequences of that decision. He argues that the remarkable freedom available to white Virginians of all classes during that time was built on the fact that black people were enslaved.

Allan Nevins and Henry Steele Commager, *A Pocket History of the United States*. 6th ed. New York: Pocket Books, 1976. A one-volume overview of American history; generally gives clear though brief perspectives of events and controversies.

Solomon Northup, *Twelve Years a Slave*. Buffalo: Miller, Orton, and Mulligan, 1854. Northup was a free black man who was kidnapped and sold into slavery. This book is one of the most reliable accounts of slavery from a slave perspective.

Stephen B. Oates, *With Malice Toward None*. New York: New American Library, 1981. Called the best one-volume biography of Abraham Lincoln ever written, this book presents Lincoln's feelings about slavery and the slavery question with remarkable clarity.

Louis Ruchames, *The Abolitionists: A Collection of Their Writings*. New York: G.P. Putnam's Sons, 1963. A collection of primary source documents pertaining to the abolitionists and their beliefs.

Kenneth Stampp, *The Peculiar Institution*. New York: Vintage Books, 1956. A groundbreaking study of slavery; among the first serious histories to examine slavery more from the perspective of the slaves than the owners.

P.J. Staudenraus, *The African Colonization Movement 1816–1865*. New York: Columbia University Press, 1961. A thorough account of the colonization movement: its supporters, its opponents, and the controversies it sparked on both sides.

John L. Thomas, *Slavery Attacked: The Abolitionist Crusade.* Englewood Cliffs, NJ: Prentice-Hall, 1965. A collection of abolitionist documents. The selection includes references to slave revolts, colonization, immediate emancipation, and many more abolitionist arguments.

INDEX

ABOUT THE AUTHOR

Stephen Currie is the author of more than thirty books and many magazine articles. Among his nonfiction titles are *Adoption, Issues in Sports*, and *Life in a Wild West Show* all for Lucent Books, and *We Have Marched Together: The Working Children's Crusade*. He is also a first and second grade teacher. He grew up in Chicago, where he spent many hours laboriously composing stories on an ancient manual typewriter, and now lives in Poughkeepsie, New York, with his wife, Amity, and two children, Irene and Nicholas.